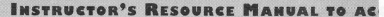
INSTRUCTOR'S RESOURCE MANUAL TO ACCOMPANY

THE WRITER'S WORKPLACE
SIXTH EDITION

AND

THE WRITER'S WORKPLACE
WITH READINGS
FOURTH EDITION

SANDRA SCARRY
Formerly with the Office of Academic Affairs, *City University of New York*

JOHN SCARRY
Hostos Community College, City University of New York

Prepared by
J'Laine Robnolt
Westark College

HARCOURT COLLEGE PUBLISHERS

Fort Worth   Philadelphia   San Diego   New York   Orlando   Austin   San Antonio

Toronto   Montreal   London   Sydney   Tokyo

Address for Domestic Orders
Harcourt College Publishers, 6277 Sea Harbor Drive, Orlando, FL 32887-6777
800-782-4479

Address for International Orders
International Customer Service
Harcourt, Inc., 6277 Sea Harbor Drive, Orlando, FL 32887-6777
407-345-3800
(fax) 407-345-4060
(e-mail) hbintl@harcourt.com

Address for Editorial Correspondence
Harcourt College Publishers, 301 Commerce Street, Suite 3700,
Fort Worth, TX 76102

Web Site Address
http://www.harcourtcollege.com

Printed in the United States of America

3 4 5 6 7 8 9 0   02

Harcourt College Publishers

Preface

The Instructor's Resource Manual to accompany *The Writer's Workplace with Readings,* fourth edition, offers numerous exercises, classroom activities, sample course outlines, chapter overviews, handouts, transparency masters, sample student paragraphs, essays, memos, and business letters that are intended to complement, reinforce, and enhance your students' experience with the primary text. Additionally, the manual provides instructors with in-depth advice on using tutors in the classroom, creating electronic portfolios, orchestrating collaborative techniques, and helping student writers use computers and the Internet. This manual was designed with the overriding goal of helping the developmental writing instructor on as many levels as possible so that he or she will have more time to devote to students.

In this edition, I have taken the liberty, when I deemed it useful, to share insights from my own experience of using *The Writer's Workplace with Readings* with my writing students over the course of eight semesters. These examples are anecdotal, and your results may differ from my own; however, I hope that an authentic account might prove helpful to some instructors.

I wish to thank Michell Phifer at Harcourt who has gone above and beyond in her patience and support throughout each stage of the project. Words cannot express the depth of my thanks to Sandra and John Scarry for their remarkable text and for their enthusiasm and insights for this manual. Also, I wish to express my appreciation to Marla Dinchak (Glendale Community College), Saad Al Kahtani (Indiana University of Pennsylvania), Tom Gier (University of Alaska at Anchorage), Karen Hancock (University of Alaska at Anchorage), Dick Harrington (Piedmont Virginia Community College), Patricia I. Mulcahy-Ernt (University of Bridgeport), and Joanne Rein, who have shared their excellent instructional articles and expertise.

I would like to express my heartfelt appreciation for the hundreds of students at Westark College, West Chester University, University of Arkansas, Temple University, and Camden County College who helped develop and revise the exercises found in the manual and who have supported my efforts for creating new activities over the years. I especially want to thank students Heather Bridges, Rossano Cherubini, Michael Hadley, Josie Heyman, Jolina Johnson, Daniel Wolbert, and Malona Zolliecoffer of Westark College who generously allowed their essays to be included in the manual and who were wonderful assets to our classes together.

I am profoundly grateful for the many friends, colleagues, and administrators at Westark College who daily demonstrate their unflagging commitment to our students and learning: President Joel Stubblefield, Dr. Sandi Sanders, Dr. Carol Raney, Zanette Douglas, Terri Leins, Robert Lowrey, Connie Phillips, Diana Rowden, Ray Watson, Linda Wetzel, and the members of the College of Learning and Academic Success and the Gordon Kelly Learning Assistance Center. Their unparalleled creativity and farsighted mission have made it possible to pilot many of the activities found in the manual.

During the course of writing this manual, I experienced the loss of my mother, Dorothy Harris Robnolt, after her valiant two-year battle with ovarian cancer. I dedicate this work in memory of her life of teaching and learning and to the bright future of my daughter, her only grandchild, Helena Elyse.

J'laine Robnolt
jrobnolt@westark.edu
Westark College, 2001

Introduction

Since the last edition of *The Writer's Workplace with Readings,* computer use and Internet access in the writing classroom have become an option for many instructors. Even if campus facilities are not able to accommodate the demand for computer-aided writing classes, more and more of our students have home access to both computers and the Internet. In fact, many students enter college having more computer savvy than we and expect the computer to be an integral part of their learning. On-line course offerings are becoming more abundant, and many of us are striving to rapidly retrain ourselves to stay ahead of the curve.

As a result, the new edition provides computer information, grammar Websites, writing Websites, on-line writing lab addresses, and on-line graded quizzes for your students. In addition, many interactive computer exercises that will enhance your students research skills appear at the end of each chapter. They will receive advice on writing and revising on word processing programs and see how much easier it is becoming to detect plagiarism via the Internet.

The Writer's Workplace has combined the best pedagogical methods with straightforward language, creative grammar and structured exercises, and fascinating readings. I feel confident you and your students will enjoy your experience and wish you the best of luck using this very special text.

Contents

PART ② CHAPTER GUIDE FOR *THE WRITER'S WORKPLACE WITH READINGS,* FOURTH EDITION 35

PART ③ INSTRUCTIONAL ESSAYS 53

APPENDIX A: CLASSROOM HANDOUTS 103

Contents

An Overview of the Text

Part One, "An Invitation to Writing," is a discussion of the rudiments of the writing process, concentrating on different types of idea-generating strategies, summarizing, paraphrasing, journaling, creating surveys, and conducting interviews. The elements of writing—Prewriting, Audience, Unity, Coherence, and Purpose—are covered in detail in Chapter 2. Students are presented with a microcosm of the writing process from idea generation and invention to editing and proofreading final drafts.

In Part Two, "Creating Effective Sentences," students are directed through a series of chapters on grammar and punctuation topics that steadily increase in complexity. Students will find that the focus is on mastering the grammar and mechanics essential for their success as writers in both the academic and business environments. These chapters deal with the most common speaker/writer errors in a clearly structured format and are complete with exercises that reinforce the learning of each new skill.

Part Three, "Understanding the Power of Words," encourages students to pay close attention to style and word choice. It also provides ample exercise in distinguishing between look-alike and sound-alike words. The exercises in "Choosing Words That Work" focus on helping students acquire a "feel" for the effect their written word choices will have on a reading audience; the chapter also stresses the importance of good writing choices, revising, and editing. "Paying Attention to Look-Alikes and Sound-Alikes" shows students the detrimental effects of common mistakes.

Part Four, "Creating Effective Paragraphs," prepares students for writing full-length academic essays by introducing them to the ideas of topic sentences, controlling ideas, and supporting details. It then furthers their writing development by directing them to create complex paragraphs using rhetorical modes.

In Part Five, "Structuring the College Essay," students will have the opportunity to put all of these skills toward the creation of standard-length college essays while continuing to hone their grammar, usage, and stylistic abilities. Students will analyze several student essays for the purpose of developing better editing and proofreading skills. Each successive chapter exercises the students' repertoire of rhetorical skills by guiding them through the process of writing full-length essays. After writing narrative, process, comparison/contrast, and/or persuasive essays, the student will have acquired the necessary tools to write effective college-level essays.

Each chapter of *The Writer's Workplace* is concluded with a "Working Together" exercise for the purpose of involving students in group endeavors. Additionally, Internet exercises are suggested in every "Working Together" to give students the opportunity to build strong computer literacy and research skills.

A helpful appendix of parts of speech, irregular verbs, and spelling is a quick resource for students. In this edition, computer boxes with suggested Websites and computer advice have been placed strategically throughout the text to reinforce students' awareness of the wealth of additional information available from any computer with Internet access. In the last section of the text, a wide range of reading selections, many of them new, are certain to spark productive class discussion and provide excellent models for their writing.

An Overview of the Instructor's Manual

Part I of this manual contains in-depth information, exercises, and examples in five areas: grading, syllabus preparation, writing skills, journaling, reading skills, and study skills. You will find the following:

- a writing proficiency grading rubric,
- suggestions for your syllabus,
- sample course outlines,
- journal grading suggestions,
- journal exercises,
- advice on presenting readings,
- reading activities,
- a sample reading quiz,
- study skill activities,
- a sample library resource quiz,
- suggestions for writing assignment requirements,
- paragraph and essay writing prompts,
- and revision suggestions.

Part II is a chapter guide to *The Writer's Workplace with Readings,* 4e, and includes rhetorical mode activities, writing process activities, and group activities.

In Part III, the following essays by respected peers have been included:

- "Collaboration in the Developmental Writing Classroom" by Dick Harrington,
- "Using the World Wide Web to Create a Learner-Centered Classroom" by Marla Dinchak,
- "Incorporating Computer Literacy into the Composition Classroom" by Joanne Rein,
- "Portfolios as a Part of the Developmental Writing Classroom" by Patricia I. Mulcahy-Ernt,
- "Electronic Portfolios in ESL Writing: An Alternative Approach" by Saad Al Kahtani,
- "Using Tutors in a Developmental Writing Class" by Karan Hancock and Tom Gier.

Appendix A provides classroom handouts. Appendix B provides sample student paragraphs, essays, memos, and business letters. Appendix C provides handouts for peer critiquing and essay grading, sample exams, and a mid-term class evaluation, and a student permission form. Finally, Appendix D provides transparency masters that cover the main ideas of Chapters 1–12.

Using the Handouts, Transparency Masters, Evaluation Handouts, and Sample Student Writings in the Appendices

The following are some suggestions for using the appended materials to enhance your work with *The Writer's Workplace*.

The handouts in Appendix A correspond with material in Chapters 13–31 and can be used to reinforce students' work in those chapters. The handouts cover connotation, sound-alike words, and the rhetorical modes. Most of the handouts ask students to complete a given task that can be accomplished during class if time allows or at home for further skill reinforcement. You may wish to grade the handouts or have students compare work with one another. Tell students that all handout exercises are to be saved in the pockets of their journals or in a manila folder for future reference.

Appendix B contains many student paragraphs, essays, memos, and business letters. Students are understandably curious about how other students write: in fact, student writers often make better models for developmental writers than professional writers, whose accomplishment seems unattainable. Some of the samples in this appendix could be considered models while others are in need of some type of revision.

The peer and instructor writing evaluation handouts in Appendix C are designed to help students receive feedback on their writing, which identifies problem areas, praises and encourages successful aspects, and provides a series of guideposts in the portfolio or process writing model. The handouts can be copied directly from the manual and given to students to attach to each essay, writing project, and revision over the course of the term. The peer writing evaluation handouts not only provide writers with new perspectives on their written work but also give student readers a guide for becoming successful critics. This section also provides two sample exams.

The transparency masters in Appendix D cover the main ideas of Chapters 1–12 (chapters dealing with the writing process, grammar, and mechanics) in *The Writer's Workplace*. They reinforce the chapter reading students are asked to do over the course of Parts I and II; also, the transparencies may be helpful as visual aids to your own lectures. The masters are designed to be photocopied directly onto transparent slides to be used on overhead projectors in the classroom. If you have access to PowerPoint or other presentation programs, you may wish to translate the material on the masters into simple computer presentations. When it comes time to review for an exam, you may want to copy the masters for students to use as study guides.

Curriculum Planning and Grading

About Grading and the Syllabus

Decisions about grading should be firmly rooted in your philosophy of writing. Grading criteria should be clearly set out in the syllabus and course outline. Rationales for grades of A through F should be made clear in order to minimize students' complaints and ensure fairness. Models of good writing should be used frequently throughout the course. It is helpful to show students examples of final or exit exams that received specific grades. If it is not possible to present entire essays, provide model paragraphs to give students a better idea of expectations of their writing. Model essays and/or paragraphs are more useful to students than lists describing the elements of good writing.

If you are new to teaching, your mentor or department chairs should be able to provide you with copies of graded essays that have been used in the preceding semesters. Otherwise, you can ask a colleague who has kept student papers written in the past. Students appreciate seeing both extremes, the exemplary A paper and the failure paper. Ideally, they should see copies of what has received grades of A, B, C, and D. Even though these are end-of-the-semester examples, they go a long way in also showing students what the writing course will be about.

Peter Elbow has written a cogent article on the paradoxes in the teaching process. Some of the contradictions instructors encounter include the following:

1. We are caught between our commitment to knowledge/society and our commitment to our students.

2. We are asked to be both guardians (coaches) and bouncers.

3. We discriminate, evaluate, test, grade, and certify, yet we must also aid, abet, guard, protect, cherish, motivate, and praise.

4. We finish as critical gatekeepers but begin as motivators, facilitators, mentors, and guides.

5. We want to teach students one kind of writing while being impelled by our understanding of the writing process to teach another way.

6. We can't expect students to volunteer weaknesses and problems when we have the job of judging and awarding them a grade.

But the bottom line is that grades and credits must do justice to knowledge and society's standards for truth. Peter Elbow states, "I am not just talking about how to serve students and serve the knowledge of society. I am also talking about developing opposite and complementary sides of our character and personality: the supportive and nurturing side and the tough, demanding side. I submit that we all have instincts and needs of both sorts. The gentlest, softest, and most flexible among us really need a chance to stick up for our latent tight standards, and the most hawkeyed, critical minded bouncers at the bar of civilization among us really need a chance to use our nurturing and supportive muscles instead of always being an adversary."

As you write your syllabus and course outline, keep in mind:

1. You are going to administer a grade at finals.
2. You must judge as fairly as you can all the aspects of a student's work and competence.
3. You will have to remember that whenever you grade a student's paper, you may have to defend your grading decisions to that student.
4. You want to be as explicit and detailed as possible, not just at the beginning of the semester but at all the points in between, including the juncture where you might have to counsel a student about the fact that it is in his or her best interest to drop the course.
5. You may find yourself in a position of being asked to justify a grade you've given a student to a supervisor or dean.
6. You will want to clarify your decision on a contested grade as much as you can in writing to convince an administrator, parent, student, or yourself.
7. You want to convince students that your class is "doable"; that they will be comfortable with the demands as printed in your syllabus.
8. You want to be certain that your standards and assessment match those of your colleagues in your department.

In summary, your grading policy should be written in clear and precise language. It should be spelled out in more ways than one. References to grading should be frequent. Your policy should be elucidated and meted out fairly so that there is no question or confusion.

What Your Students Need to Know About Proficiency Exams

1. It would be a rare occasion if a student made it through both college and life without having to prove his writing competence on a surprise topic or choice of topics.
2. Students should prepare for this possibility on proficiency exams in order to minimize anxiety.
3. Students should understand that readers know that all writers write differently, that they will probably not be forced into a rhetorical mode or particular design.
4. Almost all writing needs to have many supporting details and examples, to make a point, and to have a clear thesis sentence which answers the topic.
5. Students should check and recheck as they go along to make sure they are staying on topic.
6. Freewriting, outlining, brainstorming, and clustering can all usually be done on scratch paper.

7. Slower writers and/or ESL students need to be counseled to write less and edit more because it is competency in finding and correcting errors that often places them in a lower level.

8. Although they will not have the chance to revise at home or have the benefit of musing time, they are usually allowed to use a dictionary. Students can brainstorm and use the dictionary to solve writer's block.

9. Worldwide, the single writing product is considered a valid measure of students' development and ability to logically support a point in an organized and coherent way with a minimum of errors.

10. Writing performance is an effective measure of whether students have mastered and can apply the instruction that they have received in class.

11. All this said, there is usually an appeals process.

Writing Proficiency Exams—A Sample Rubric

The following rubric can be adapted to your classes' or department's needs easily. Many colleges and universities have established holistic entrance and exit exams for writing and English students. Of those I have participated in, scales of either 1–4 (with 4 being the highest score) or 1–6 (with 6 being the highest score) were used rather that the standard A–F. By using an even number of possible scores, faculty were forced to make tough judgments between essays that would normally fall into the "C" category and decide if those essays were, in fact, essentially upper level "C's" (competent) or lower level "C's" (not competent). Each essay was blind-read by two faculty members, unless their scores differed by more than two scoring levels. In that event, a third faculty tie-break reader scored the essay. There are many models of holistic grading, and each department will design the one which best fits its student population.

Using a scale from 1–6 where 6 is the highest score a student can receive, a breakdown of general criteria for each score might be as follows:

A score of 6—The essay provides a well-organized response to the topic and maintains a central focus. The ideas are expressed in appropriate language. A sense of pattern of development is present from beginning to end. The writer supports assertions with explanations or illustrations, and the vocabulary is well suited to the context. Sentences reflect a command of syntax within the ordinary range of standard written English. Grammar, punctuation, and spelling are almost always correct.

A score of 5—The essay provides an organized response to the topic. The ideas are expressed in clear language most of the time. The writer develops ideas and generally signals relationships within and between paragraphs. The writer uses vocabulary that is appropriate for the essay topic and avoids oversimplifications or distortions. Sentences generally are correct grammatically, although some errors may be present when sentence structure is particularly complex. With few exceptions, grammar, punctuation, and spelling are correct.

A score of 4—The essay shows a basic understanding of the demands of essay organization, although there may be occasional digressions. The development of ideas may be sometimes incomplete, but a basic, logical structure is apparent. Vocabulary is generally appropriate for the essay topic, but at times it is oversimplified. Sentences reflect a sufficient command of standard written English to ensure reasonable clarity of expression. Common forms of agreement and grammatical inflection are usually, although not always, correct. The writer generally demonstrates through punctuation an understanding of the boundaries of the sentence. The writer spells common words, except so-called "demons" (e.g., their, there, they're), with a reasonable degree of accuracy.

A score of 3—The essay (or paragraph) responds to the topic and shows some structure. The main idea is discernible and is developed, not merely repeated. The writer uses informal language occasionally and records conversational speech when appropriate academic prose is needed. Vocabulary is limited. The writer signals relationships within paragraphs. Syntax may be rudimentary and lacking in variety. The essay has some grammatical problems, or because of an extremely narrow range of syntactical choices, only occasional grammatical problems appear. The writer may not demonstrate a consistent understanding of the boundaries of the sentence. The writer occasionally misspells common words.

A score of 2—The essay begins with a response to the topic but does not develop that response. Ideas are repeated frequently, or are presented randomly, or both. The writer uses informal language frequently and does little more than record conversational speech. Words are often misused, and vocabulary is limited. Syntax is often tangled and is not sufficiently stable to ensure reasonable clarity of expression. Errors in grammar, punctuation, and spelling occur often.

A score of 1—The essay suffers from general incoherence and has no discernible pattern of organization. It displays a high frequency of error in the regular features of standard written English. Lapses in punctuation, spelling, and grammar often frustrate the reader. Or, the essay is so brief that any reasonably accurate judgment of the writer's competence is impossible.

How to Use the Sample Syllabi

The following syllabi look similar, but on closer inspection you will see that they are quite different. Both are "real" syllabi from my previous semesters working with the text, which I thought might be more helpful than "mock ups." When developing your own syllabus, strive for an eclectic and progressive approach. Integrate writing, grammar, and readings in stages of complexity.

The sixteen-week syllabus uses the portfolio approach to student writing. The final weeks of the course are focused entirely on rewriting, editing, and critiquing. You can easily adapt the syllabus for a half semester course by doubling up. The six-week (summer) syllabus appears to be a whirlwind, and it is. Due to the intensity of meeting nearly every day for long periods, students retain the material better from class to class, which enables us to move quickly. A portfolio approach was not used in this class, and paragraph writing and grammar were more highly stressed than essay writing since it was the lower level of two levels of developmental writing in our curriculum. This syllabus can also be adapted to twelve-week tri-terms by dividing each class period.

Sample Course Outlines

Conduct of Course for a Sixteen-Week Semester
UNIT ONE: "GIT IT WRIT. THEN GET IT RIGHT."
GETTING STARTED, BUILDING CONFIDENCE, CREATING A WRITING EN-
VIRONMENT, BECOMING A GOOD WRITER, AND DEVELOPING EDITING
SKILLS
(THE STAGES OF WRITING)

Week One

T Introduction to course and explanation of the syllabus. A diagnostic writing
will be administered.

R *The Writer's Workplace* Chapter 1. Notebook with 5 labeled sections (Class
Notes, Working Journal, Personal Journal, Commonplace Book, Writing As-
signment Corrections/Vocabulary, Notes) due. Read "Freewriting" by Peter
Elbow, and be prepared for discussion.

Week Two

T We will have an in-class visit with a passionate reader. Read "Summer Reading" by Michael Dorris. *The Writer's Workplace* Chapter 16; Rough draft of
paragraph due. In-class writing on a narrative piece from a book-on-tape.

R *The Writer's Workplace* Chapter 15 due. In-class peer editing of the second
draft of paragraph assignment.

UNIT TWO: "PAINTING WITH WORDS"
CREATING VERBAL PORTRAITS OF PEOPLE, PLACES, AND THINGS
(DESCRIPTION)

Week Three

T *The Writer's Workplace* Chapters 2 and 17 due. Paragraph description of a
photograph due. In-class visit with a visual artist.

R *The Writer's Workplace* Chapter 3. Report on artist's visit due. Paragraph
with supporting details due. Exam over subjects and verbs in second half of
class.

Week Four

T *The Writer's Workplace* Chapter 20. Read "The Paterson Public Library" by
Judith Ortiz Cofer.

R Paragraphs describing a person or a place due. *The Writer's Workplace* Chapter 13 will be covered in class.

UNIT THREE: "HAVE I EVER TOLD YOU THE ONE ABOUT . . ."
TELLING STORIES SO THEY'RE ON THE EDGE OF THEIR SEATS
(NARRATIVE)

Week Five

T In-class visit with a published writer. *The Writer's Workplace* Chapter 19 due.

R Report on writer's visit due. *The Writer's Workplace* Chapter 5 due. Read "My
Daughter Smokes" by Alice Walker.

Week Six

T *The Writer's Workplace* Chapter 6 due.

R Narrative paragraph due. *The Writer's Workplace* Chapter 13 will be covered in class. Exam over fragments in second half of class.

UNIT FOUR: "FIRST YOU TAKE THE PEANUTS AND YOU SMASH 'EM . . ."
EXPLAINING HOW AND HOW COME
(PROCESS)

Week Seven

T *The Writer's Workplace* Chapters 7 and 21 due. Review for midterm exam.

R Midterm exam.

Week Eight

T *The Writer's Workplace* Chapter 8 due.

R Process paragraph due. *The Writer's Workplace* Chapter 11 will be covered in class. Exam over run-ons and comma splices in second half of class.

UNIT FIVE: "FOR BETTER OR WORSE . . ."
EVALUATING TWO SUBJECTS FOR A REASON
(COMPARISON/CONTRAST)

Week Nine

T *The Writer's Workplace* Chapter 22 and Chapter 30 due.

R Read "Dream Houses" by Tenaya Darlington and "Neat People vs. Sloppy People" by Suzanne Britt. *The Writer's Workplace* Chapter 10 due.

Week Ten

T *The Writer's Workplace* Chapter 32 due. In-class writing exam over paragraphs will be taken during the class period.

R Comparison/Contrast essay due. *The Writer's Workplace* Chapter 9 will be covered in class.

UNIT SIX: "STEERING AROUND SLIPPERY SLOPES, POISON WELLS, AND STRAW MEN"
CONVINCING THE FENCE-SITTERS WITHOUT PREACHING TO THE CHOIR
(PERSUASION)

Week Eleven

T *The Writer's Workplace* Chapter 31 due.

R *The Writer's Workplace* Chapter 12 due. Read "Online but Not Antisocial" by Janna Malamud Smith and "The Issue Isn't Sex, It's Violence" by Caryl Rivers.

Week Twelve

T Persuasive essay due.

UNIT SEVEN: "NOW, GET IT RIGHT"
PEER EDITING AND YOUR PORTFOLIO

R Peer Editing of Description Essay.

Week Thirteen

  T Peer Editing of Narrative Essay. Revised Description Essay Due.

  R Peer Editing of Narrative Essay.

Week Fourteen

  T Peer Editing of Process Essay. Revised Narrative Essay Due.

  R Peer Editing of Process Essay.

Week Fifteen

  T Peer Editing of Comparison/Contrast Essay. Revised Process Essay Due.

  R Peer Editing of Comparison/Contrast Essay.

Week Sixteen

  T Revised Comparison/Contrast Essay Due.

  R Semester Portfolios due. Review for final exam.

Conduct of Course for a Six-Week Summer Term

UNIT ONE: "GIT IT WRIT. THEN GET IT RIGHT."
GETTING STARTED, BUILDING CONFIDENCE, CREATING A WRITING ENVI-
RONMENT, BECOMING A GOOD WRITER, AND DEVELOPING EDITING SKILLS
(THE STAGES OF WRITING)

Week One

  M Introduction to course and explanation of the syllabus. In-class diagnostic writing will be administered.

  T *The Writer's Workplace* Chapter 1 due. Notebook with 5 labeled sections (Class Notes, Working Journal, Personal Journal, Commonplace Book, Writing Assignment Corrections/Vocabulary, Notes) due. Read "Freewriting" by Peter Elbow, and be prepared for discussion.

  W We will have an in-class visit with a passionate reader. Read "Summer Reading" by Michael Dorris, and be prepared for discussion. *The Writer's Workplace* Chapter 16 due; rough draft of paragraph due.

  R *The Writer's Workplace* Chapter 15 due. In-class peer editing of second draft of paragraph assignment will be done in the second half of class.

UNIT TWO: "PAINTING WITH WORDS"
CREATING VERBAL PORTRAITS OF PEOPLE, PLACES, AND THINGS
(DESCRIPTION)

Week Two

  M *The Writer's Workplace* Chapters 2 and 17 due. Description of a photograph due. We will have an in-class visit with a visual artist.

  T *The Writer's Workplace* Chapter 3 due. Report on artist's visit due. Paragraph with supporting details due.

  W *The Writer's Workplace* Chapter 20 due. Read "The Paterson Public Library" by Judith Ortiz Cofer, and be prepared for discussion.

  R Paragraphs describing a person or a place due. *The Writer's Workplace* Chapter 13 will be covered in class. Exam over subjects and verbs will be administered in the second half of class.

UNIT THREE: "HAVE I EVER TOLD YOU THE ONE ABOUT . . ."
TELLING STORIES SO THEY'RE ON THE EDGE OF THEIR SEATS
(NARRATIVE)

Week Three

M   We will have an in-class visit with a published writer. *The Writer's Workplace* Chapter 19 due.

T   Report on writer's visit due. *The Writer's Workplace* Chapter 5 due. Read "My Daughter Smokes" by Alice Walker, and be prepared for discussion.

W   *The Writer's Workplace* Chapter 6 due.

R   Narrative Paragraph due. *The Writer's Workplace* Chapter 14 will be covered in class. Exam over fragments will be administered in second half of class.

UNIT FOUR: "FIRST YOU TAKE THE PEANUTS AND YOU SMASH 'EM . . ."
EXPLAINING HOW AND HOW COME
(PROCESS)

Week Four

M   *The Writer's Workplace* Chapter 21 due.

T   *The Writer's Workplace* Chapter 7 due.

W   *The Writer's Workplace* Chapter 8 due.

R   Process Paragraph due. *The Writer's Workplace* Chapter 11 will be covered in class. Exam over run-ons and comma splices will be administered in the second half of class.

UNIT FIVE: "FOR BETTER OR WORSE . . ."
EVALUATING TWO SUBJECTS FOR A REASON
(COMPARISON/CONTRAST)

Week Five

M   *The Writer's Workplace* Chapter 23 and Chapter 30 due.

T   Read "Neat People vs. Sloppy People" by Suzanne Britt and "Dream Houses" by Tenaya Darlington. *The Writer's Workplace* Chapter 10 due.

W   *The Writer's Workplace* Chapter 32 due. Exam over paragraphs will be taken during the class period.

R   Comparison/Contrast essay due. *The Writer's Workplace* Chapter 9 will be covered in class.

UNIT SIX: "STEERING AROUND SLIPPERY SLOPES, POISON WELLS, AND STRAW MEN"
CONVINCING THE FENCE-SITTERS WITHOUT PREACHING TO THE CHOIR
(PERSUASION)

Week Six

M   *The Writer's Workplace* Chapter 31 due.

T   *The Writer's Workplace* Chapter 12 due. Read "Online but Not Antisocial" by Janna Malamud Smith and "The Issue Isn't Sex, It's Violence" by Caryl Rivers, and be prepared for discussion.

W   Persuasive essay due. We will review for final exam.

R   Final Exam. The final will consist of two parts: a grammar exam and an in-class writing assignment. You must pass both halves of the exam with at least a score of 75 percent in order to pass the course.

Writing Skills

Guiding Reluctant Writers Through the Writing Process Using Portfolios

Some instructors are reluctant to use a more process-oriented model in their classrooms because the amount of grading appears to be staggering. Although there are many stages to the writing process, few of these stages need to receive actual grades, and many students flourish with a mix of thoughtful feedback, peer critiques, and grades. Therefore, if you orchestrate the stages of the process and allow students to take responsibility for critiquing some of those stages, you may find your workload decreased rather than increased. The following is one of many possible breakdowns of the writing process which works quite well in the writing classroom. (For an in-depth discussion of the portfolio, please refer to "Portfolios as a Part of the Developmental Writing Classroom" by Patricia I. Mulcahy-Ernt in Part III.)

Choosing a Topic

This stage of the process sounds deceptively simple; yet, failing to master the skill of tailoring a topic to something interesting has been the downfall of many writers. Students may not realize that they should write about topics that matter to them and that no one else will be interested in what they write if they themselves find it overly simple or boring. Have students do the initial work of choosing their topics in class the first few times you meet so you may check their progress and help them use invention strategies to spur their memories and imaginations.

Show students an example of topic development on the board. First, pick a general topic that appears to be boring: the current political climate, the change in life expectancy in the last one hundred years, team sports, etc. In fact, even though it does not matter what topic you choose, students are impressed when they see a topic generally thought of as "boring" transformed into an exciting-sounding topic sentence or thesis. Then through clustering, listing, or freewriting, show students how these topics could become "What's So Good About Nasty Campaign Ads?"; "What Will You Do With the Last 100 Years of Your Life?"; and "How Free Agency Is Destroying Baseball as We Love It." Walk through another seemingly boring topic as a group. Don't end the exercise until you sense that you have "gotten somewhere interesting." Next, give another topic prompt, and have the students work on creating an interesting topic sentence or thesis statement on their own as you walk around the room and help them individually. Finally, suggest that a student should brainstorm on several topics before deciding which one he or she will write the essay about.

Using Invention Strategies to Great Effect

Once all of your students have created a topic sentence or thesis for their paragraph or essay assignment, allow ten to twenty minutes of class time to practice using any combination of invention strategies; then survey their work to see if they are coming up with a range of ideas and signs of interesting supporting details, examples, facts, and so on, which will make writing the rough draft easier. You may consider giving students time to freewrite for ten minutes every class period—sometimes on essay topics, sometimes on issues brought up in the readings—in order to hone these crucial skills.

Thesis Narrowing

Out of the students' invention stage should come a roughly narrowed thesis. Stress that it will waste their valuable time to write a rough draft with a thesis or topic sentence that has not been sufficiently narrowed. Since students sometimes find it easier to critique classmates' work rather than their own, ask them to exchange journals with a partner and give and receive commentary on the proposed thesis or topic sentence. They might further explain what they hope to discuss in the essay and give examples of supporting detail they plan to employ.

Drafting to Relieve Writer's Block

Sometimes, even after narrowing a thesis, a writer does not really know what he or she thinks about an issue until a substantial amount of writing has been completed. For this reason, you may wish to implement the "Exploration Draft" as one of the stages you require. The advantages are two-fold: students receive additional writing practice which will be evaluated by their peers rather than you, and, when the rough drafts are submitted, they are generally more polished than they would be otherwise. Tell students that the exploration draft is little more than a focused freewriting opportunity and that they should fill up approximately two to three notebook pages. Their goal should be to discover what they think about the topic they have chosen and to detect evidence of a side issue that might be far more interesting to them than their initial thesis.

Peer Evaluating of Earliest Drafts

Students typically make wonderful evaluators for exploration drafts—they tend to be encouraging and supportive in exactly the right amounts. In fact, negativity and criticism have no place at this stage. Every beginning writer can benefit from statements often heard during peer critiques, "No, this is really good!" and "Don't be ridiculous—of course you can write." To make the evaluation process move along and stay focused, give evaluation sheets to the students with a series of basic questions to answer about the draft they are evaluating. When these sheets are completed, they must be turned in to the student writer who will keep it in his or her portfolio.

Writing the Rough Draft

Students are well prepared for writing the rough draft at this point. This will be the first stage to receive an actual grade. When you encounter a usage error or some other kind of mistake, draw a dash by the line in which the error occurs and make a hash mark on the "Mechanics and Usage Errors" sheet. Not only will this save you time, the method forces students to figure out their errors and use their own resources to correct them. Additionally, the point breakdown sheet gives students a great deal of guidance toward their revisions. It also shows how they may have earned a low score rather than accepting "That's what I always get." Staple both sheets to each student paper, or give students the sheets at the semester's start and require them to staple the sheets to the paper prior to submission.

Proofreading and High-level Editing

You may wish to have students revise their essays once before this stage and have another round of peer review. Once you are satisfied that the students are within reach of a final draft, you may give them the task of condensing their essays by half a page by deleting empty words and phrases, redundancies, interjections, and by subordinating less important information. You might have students exchange papers and, if it is an essay assignment, underline the thesis and all topic sentences. Students might be required to edit one paragraph of another student's paper. Notice that students are honing all of their critical skills through peer work.

Writing the "Final Draft"

Students are usually amazed to hear of writers who are not satisfied with their work until they have completed forty or more drafts. Perhaps there is no such thing as a Platonic final draft—and even if there is, the concept of a "final" draft leaves out the concept of writing as discovery and conversation. When you grade the-last-revision-of-the-paper-that-you-will-see, you will attend to several matters that were of less concern in previous drafts. You will probably not give students as many points for grammar and usage, given the amount of time they have had to work out the kinks. You will be looking for paragraph unity and coherence, and for improvement of style, details, and focus. You might remind students that any deficiencies should be eliminated before submitting the portfolio at the semester's end.

The Student Portfolio

At the semester's end, students may be required to submit the final drafts of all their course work in a folder for a portfolio grade. Some instructors allow students to leave the weakest paper out of the portfolio while another method might be to have each student choose his or her three best papers.

If you do elect to use the portfolio method, you might assign a final writing assignment to be included in the portfolio in which students evaluate their writing progress over the term, detailing what they have learned and identifying areas that still need improvement. They might be asked to describe their personal experience with the writing process, or they might analyze the essays in their portfolios in terms of guidelines that you choose.

Whatever method you decide to use with portfolios in your classroom, one thing is clear: by following and checking student progress at every stage, you will have a much better impression of each student's writing progress and certainty that the work is original.

Assigning Home Writing

You will probably find that students starting their basic writing studies will have difficulty producing standard two-and-one-half page, typed, double-spaced home writing assignments. Make it your goal to prepare each student for this common English department standard by the end of the term. To accomplish this, increase the length and complexity of the assignments as students gain confidence and the required skills. Sometimes instructors, in an attempt to appear welcoming, give students too little direction. In the beginning, however, students generally need a good deal more structure for their writing assignments. Therefore, avoid giving students assignments with a general expectation such as, "Write a two-page story" or "Talk about a process you know something about." This harms the tentative writer who needs guidelines to follow in order to feel that success is possible. Be specific about length and content expectations while remaining flexible. One possible scheme for building students' writing stamina over the semester follows:

Paragraph Assignments: Require four to six typed (or neatly handwritten and double-spaced on lined notebook paper, if you are willing) home writing assignments. Students should become habituated to revising the errors in their work from the beginning, but increasingly with each assigned writing you may require more attention paid to correcting structural deficiencies in their paragraphs, using sufficient supporting detail, and employing appropriate transitional words and phrases. Around midterm, you might start to attach a checklist to each of the students' drafts to encourage them to satisfy these requirements.

Essay Assignments: If your college or university has a computer lab, you may wish at this point to ban all handwritten home writing assignments. Require two or three home essay assignments. The structure of each assignment will probably center on a different rhetorical mode as you cover them in the text. You may also challenge the students to respond to specific readings in some or all of their papers. The initial essay assignments should be at least over one full page in length, with the final assignment two and one-half pages long. Expect students to adopt a more sophisticated attitude toward revision at this stage and have them revise some or all of their essays more than once. Not all of these drafts need to receive a grade, merely peer feedback (see section entitled "Guiding Reluctant Writers Through the Writing Process Using Portfolios"; also see "Peer Evaluation for Exploration Draft" handout). The first revision receives a peer critique. The next revision, submitted for a grade, concentrates on style, word choice, and fluidity of language. You might, for example, require the second revision to be a half page shorter than the previous drafts in order to encourage the editing of empty words, phrases, and sentences. The final drafts may be submitted in a folder, with or without previous drafts, at the semester's end.

Writing Prompts

1. In-Class Diagnostic Writing Assignment: *Describe a Place*
   Describe your favorite place to go on vacation or on the weekend.
   Don't leave out any details of the place that you like. Try to use all the senses (Touch: what does the weather feel like? Taste: what do you eat while you're there? Smell: are there any odors or fragrances? Hearing: what are some things you might hear? Sight: look at everything in minute detail—what do you see?)

   Suggestions for Revision:
   Reread your piece several times. Notice whether you have described your place from left to right, top to bottom, or any other clear ordering. If you have not, reorganize your details to help your reader's mental eye "see" the details flow from one to the other.

2. In-Class Writing Assignment: *Analyze an Advertisement*
   You will be given a magazine advertisement by your instructor. Take time to read the copy and study the visual. Try to answer the following questions: Who is the ad trying to reach? How do you know this? What elements are present in the visual which would make it appealing to people of that group, in your opinion? What choice of words is interesting or unusual? Is the ad on the whole persuasive?

When you have analyzed these aspects, write an essay no less than five paragraphs in length which explains the persuasive tactics of the ad.

Suggestions for Revision:
When you review your work, underline the topic sentence in each paragraph. If there is no one sentence that can stand as the topic sentence, you probably need to do some thinking about the focus of the paragraph and rewrite accordingly. Do all of the sentences in each paragraph pertain to its topic sentence? Is the language interesting? Would someone who had never seen the advertisement be able to understand what you are writing about?

3. Home Writing Assignment: *Analyze an Ad Campaign*
Analyze the persuasive techniques of 1.) a single advertising campaign using a minimum of five different ads from current magazines or 2.) a minimum of five ads for a similar type of merchandise by rival companies. Be very specific in describing the ads, and address both the verbal and visual aspects. Submit your brainstorming notes, rough drafts, and copies of the ads with your final copy.

Suggestions for Revision:
Make sure you review the ads you chose before you begin revising. Do you notice anything new that you had not seen before? Did your draft contain a balance between the visual and the verbal? Is your presentation interesting? Does your introduction grab the reader? Does the conclusion sum up the main points and leave the reader with one or two observations?

4. Home Writing Assignment: *Write a Brief Narrative*
Make up a story with at least three people that has a beginning, a middle, and an end. See if you can make the story interesting to someone of your age group. Try having the people talk to one another.

Suggestions for Revision:
Look over your work carefully and make sure that all of your subjects and verbs agree. Ask yourself, "Does the dialogue sound natural?" "Are there enough surprises?" "Is the plot easy to understand?" Revise to make the answers to these questions yes.

5. Home Writing Assignment: *Write a Scene*
People disagree about issues all the time. Think back to an issue you have argued about with friends or family in the past. Write a scene using only dialogue that has several people arguing over an idea or issue. Remember, each person wants to be heard.

Suggestions for Revision:
Make sure that it is clear to other readers what the people in your scene are arguing about. Does each person have a distinct way of speaking or do they speak the way you do?

6. Home Writing Assignment: *Explain a Favorite Quote or Cliché*
Everyone knows a few sayings that come in handy from time to time, for example: "Never let the sun go down on your anger," "The grass is always greener on the other side of the fence," and "Don't judge someone until you have walked ten miles in his or her shoes." Choose any saying or cliché that you find interesting; first explain what it means in general and second tell what it has shown you in your own life.

Suggestions for Revision:
Review what you have written and decide if you would like to have a humorous or instructive intent. Then look for missed opportunities in your work where you can make your intent apparent.

7. Home Writing Assignment: *Write a Process*
Choose an activity you can do very well—make a pizza, hit a golf ball, drive a stick shift—and write detailed directions for a beginner to perform the same activity. Don't forget to mention from the beginning any equipment, ingredients, or special clothing that may be needed.

Suggestions for Revision:
Give your directions to someone who does not know how to perform the activity and ask whether he or she feels able to do the task based on your guidance. If not, revise your steps accordingly.

8. Home Writing Assignment: *Write an Argument*
Convince someone you care about to stop smoking, drinking, or doing any other unhealthy habit (overeating? watching television?). Persuade him or her by using reasons, facts, and statistics about the effects of the habit.

Suggestions for Revision:
Edit out any unnecessary words and phrases, especially conversational phrases such as "well," "you know," and "okay, now." Does your argument have a clear progression of points? Does it seem to attack the listener or coerce through logical argument? Keep in mind that you would rather get results than have a fight.

9. Home Writing Assignment: *Write Three Paragraphs Complete with Topic Sentences and Supporting Details*
Pick a favorite holiday and in three paragraphs persuade the reader that this holiday is the most interesting of the year. Be sure to take three distinct aspects of the holiday and support each point with rich details. Remember to include the senses.

Suggestions for Revision:
Check your writing to make sure you have good paragraph unity and that the piece as a whole is interesting and flows well.

10. Home Writing Assignment: *Write an Essay Using Examples, Illustrations, and Anecdotes*
Do some detective work and write an investigative paper on your findings: 1.) write a survey concerning a problem or an issue and administer it to at least 20 people on campus, at work, or in your neighborhood, then report on the trends indicated clearly and in detail; 2.) watch television for one week at the same time or times each day and count instances of one of the following: suggestive brand endorsements, gunplay, political or sexual references, or another category of your own devising.

Suggestions for Revision:
Count the number of illustrations your paper contains. Do you feel that you have provided enough examples to prove the points you are trying to make? Have you presented your examples clearly with plenty of supporting detail? Revise accordingly.

11. Home Writing Assignment: *Write an Essay Explaining a Process*
Tell the story of how you learned how to do an important skill in your introduction. In the body of your essay, address yourself to people who are "just like you were" and go through the steps of learning the skill in great detail. Anticipate any difficulties they might face, and encourage them by telling them about difficulties you may have had along the way. End the essay with the completion of your story from the introduction, a new story about your newfound prowess and how it gives you great satisfaction, and a call to action.

Suggestions for Revision:
When you reread your draft, decide whether or not you have written in such a way as to capture your audience's interest. Have you left out any crucial steps? Have you made the task seem more complicated than it need be? Have you used good narrative technique when telling the story?

12. Home Writing Assignment: *Write a Comparison or Contrast Essay*
Find accounts of the same newsworthy event in two different newspapers, and investigate the manner in which this event is reported. Analyze the differences in the use of language, the phrasing (and size) of the headlines, the choice of accompanying photos, etc. What is the overall impression the reader is left with after reading each? Do either of the articles persuade the reader to a certain stance by outright statements of opinion, or more subtly by using nonverbal cues? If so, what is the stance of the writer and how does he or she achieve these effects? Be very specific: quote directly from the articles and don't assume that the reader of your paper will be familiar with the articles.

Suggestions for Revision:
Reread both of the articles you chose before you begin revising. Do you still agree with your assessment of the thrust of each article, or have you changed your mind on certain points? If you have had new insights, be sure to incorporate them into the revised draft.

13. Home Writing Assignment: *Analyze a Persuasive Essay*
Analyze the strengths and weaknesses found in a current letter to the editor, taken from a local or national newspaper. Do a bit of research, by checking his or her statistics and claims, and write a letter that refutes the original by providing other arguments. Quote directly from the original.

Suggestions for Revision:
Make sure that you have addressed the issues mentioned in the original letter in a sensitive manner. State your opponent's opinion in a clear, disinterested way at the beginning and proceed to refute the points you have mentioned systematically. Look at your conclusion—have you summarized your main points and reinforced them to have optimal persuasive effect?

14. Paragraph Assignment 1: *Write a Causal Analysis*
Choose a current issue from the newspaper or your own memory, and write about the causes of a social problem such as teen pregnancy, the high school dropout rate, unemployment, pollution, etc.

Suggestions for Revision:
Think about the effects of the same topic on society, families, or ecosystems, and incorporate these effects into your revision.

15. Paragraph Assignment 2: *Define an Abstract Term*
Choose an abstract word or concept such as *truth, beauty, justice, friendship, equality, racism,* etc. Look the word up in a good dictionary and notice the root meanings of the word; next, brainstorm about the root meanings as opposed to the actual definition of the word. Then describe your experience of the word by giving concrete examples of the word in action. Also, contrast your experience with that of others. When you write the assignment attempt to bring all of these different aspects into play.

Suggestions for Revision:
Analyze what you have written and decide whether it would be interesting for others to read. If not, go back and make sure you have an easy-to-follow structure and that you have used many sharp supporting details. Have you introduced the definition in a captivating manner?

16. Paragraph Assignment 3: *Classify a General Topic*
Take a general topic such as friendship, holidays, sports, sports fans, restaurants, gardeners, neighbors, etc. and brainstorm about different categories that could be made within the topic. Write an essay that explains each of the categories you have come up with, using many good examples. Remember, you must have at least three categories.

Suggestions for Revision:
Reread your work carefully and ask yourself these questions: Are your categories true? If not, do you have a humorous intent? If you are trying to be humorous, have you maintained a consistent humorous tone throughout?

The Journal

Solving the Problems of Using the Journal

Assigning journal writing assignments for your students is a means to help them develop the "habit of writing." Ideally, the more they write, the more risks student writers will take. Although the journal should be an integral part of teaching the writing process in a developmental composition course, many instructors abandon its use either early in the semester or early in their professional careers due to several common but tenacious problems.

One of the most pernicious difficulties is that students often remain perplexed as to the types of entries they should be writing in the journal throughout the term. It is not unusual to collect journals at mid-semester and find entries beginning as follows: "I'm still not really sure what I'm supposed to be writing, but here it goes. Jennifer and I had a fight last night and I still feel bad . . ." If an instructor has not been specific as to the nature of the entries students should produce, he or she may be in the uncomfortable and invasive position at the semester's end of knowing far more about students' lives than is appropriate for an authority figure with the power to pass or fail them.

Another common complaint from instructors is that there are no guidelines for grading or judging the journal and therefore no means to coerce students to use it and take it seriously. Additionally, there seems to be no easy way to collect the journal in order to grade it—instructors I have talked to have been frustrated that after toting thirty to sixty spiral binders across campus they find no more than a collective product of ninety journal notebook pages, many of those pages revealing no more than verbatim notes copied from the board. Despite the seeming impossibility of incorporating the journal successfully based on these problems, most of these problems can actually be solved fairly simply. If you are specific about your expectations and plan carefully, you will be successful using the journal in the classroom setting.

Introducing the Journal

Suggest that students keep a large spiral-bound notebook divided into several sections: Class Notes, Working Journal, Commonplace Book, Personal Diary (optional), and Vocabulary Notes. By having them put class notes in the same book as their journal work, you can ensure that students will always have their journals when they come to class. From the beginning, while working on the "Looking at the Whole" sections, explain the importance of the journal in the development of their overall writing skills. Stress that this journal will be a constant companion throughout the course and that all class notes, brainstorms for writing assignments, handwritten rough drafts, thoughts on readings, ideas and insights will find a home in one of the sections of that journal. The object is to encourage the students to take the journal seriously from the first day and to let them know that they will be graded on the way they have used the journal by the end of the course.

A little structure is better than total freedom when it comes to giving guidelines to students. However, because the journal is an idea-generating device, you certainly do not want to regulate the kinds of thoughts and feelings that students may wish to put in it. Instead, have them judge the category to which a certain type of journal writing falls: anything related to class work should be put in Class Notes; everything related to brainstorming, creative writing, idea generation, and written journal assignments belongs in the Working Journal; quotes, cartoons, letters, thoughts for the day, and articles should be copied, pasted, or taped in the Commonplace Book; reading activities and new vocabulary based on the readings should be put in the Vocabulary section; and, finally, if you choose to include this section, any personal experiences or thoughts should be placed in the Diary section with a rubber band or paper clip closing the section for privacy.

It is advisable to expect students to produce specific journal assignments on a regular basis—weekly journal assignments can be found in the Instructor's Guide in Part II of this manual which will reinforce the chapter skills they are learning in creative ways. Additionally, you may wish to give students an approximate number of pages you expect for certain journal sections by the end of the term (e.g., 30 pages for the Working Journal, 5 pages for Vocabulary Notes, etc.). Again the goal is to provide structure and direction while leaving the content up to them.

Grading the Journal

The most difficult aspect of incorporating the journal into a composition course is finding a grading system that is fair but does not impede students' creativity. Since there are several possible grading methods, find one that is easy to execute, achieves consistent results, and maintains a high degree of objectivity. To avoid the unpleasant job of carrying a class's worth of note-books to car or office, the following three methods are designed to be ac-complished in class while students work together in groups.

Perhaps the easiest, and fairest, journal grading method uses a point sys-tem. The students receive a certain number of points for each section of the journal, and the total is then either entered in your grade book as a percent-age, or converted into the letter grade corresponding to that point range. Weight the most important parts of their journal work the most heavily. An easy example of a 100-point scale might be:

> Class notes (including in-class group work): 20 points
>
> Working Journal: 50 points
>
> Commonplace Book: 5 points
>
> Personal Diary: 5 points
>
> Vocabulary Notes: 20 points

Using this basic 100-point scale the students' totals can easily be converted into letter grades (100–90 points = A, 89–80 points = B, and so forth).

Another grading method counts pages of work for each section, taking into account the size of each student's handwriting. A student would receive an A for the following product:

> Class Notes: 15–20 pages
>
> Working Journal: at least 30 pages (including brainstorming pages)
>
> Commonplace Book: 3–5 pages
>
> Personal Diary: 5–10 pages
>
> Vocabulary Notes: 5–10 pages

The other end of the scale is a blank notebook with a few verbatim class notes scrawled across several pages which would receive an F. Decide your own range between these extremes.

A third method takes into account content rather than quantity. Have the students mark 20 pages of their finest journal work with Post-It notes or have the students photocopy and submit the pages to you in a folder. You would then judge their work as you would an essay, for signs of in-depth work, progress, creativity, and coherence. Students can receive higher marks for using parts of their brainstorming and clustering in their rough draft and so on.

Tips on Using the Journal Assignments

The following twenty-eight journal assignments strive to help students exer-cise similar skills to the ones they are learning in *The Writer's Workplace* while providing them with enough freedom to experience their ideas, beliefs, and creativity. You may wish to copy all of the exercises and have students keep them in their journals, or you may wish to give students only one assignment at a time. If assigning specific assignments to correspond to given chapters seems too rigid for your students, you may wish to leave the choice of assignment up to them and simply make a general requirement that they complete a certain number by the end of the term. (See the section in Part I entitled "Solving the Problems of Using the Journal.")

However you decide to incorporate the journal, bear in mind that the journal not only reinforces the writing skills that your students are learning in their chapter work, it also gives them the best experience in what it feels like to be a writer, to make writerly choices, and to sense that they have something they would like to say, even if no one is going to read it but themselves.

Assignments 1–14 tend to be easier and take less time to accomplish than Assignments 15–28. You may consider allowing students to use class time to do some journal work.

Journal Assignments

Journal Assignment 1   Purchase a roomy notebook with a cover that appeals to you. You may wish to get one with pocket dividers for keeping important mementos such as photos and postcards. Make sure that it is not too bulky—spiral binders are more favorable than ring binders for this reason. Divide the notebook into five sections: 1.) Class Notes, 2.) Working Journal, 3.) Commonplace Book, 4.) Personal Diary, and 5.) Vocabulary Notes.

Copy what you wrote for Chapter 1, Activity 1, into the beginning of your Working Journal. Copy what you and the class came up with for Activity 2 into your Commonplace Book. Copy what you wrote for Activity 3 into the Personal Diary. Return to your Working Journal and create a one-page cluster on the word "Summer."

Journal Assignment 2   Create a fifteen- to twenty-word crossword puzzle using your journal as scratch paper. When you have finished, copy the completed puzzle onto another sheet of paper and give it to a friend to see how well he or she is able to solve it. Hint: it is easiest to begin with your interlocking answers.

Journal Assignment 3   In your Working Journal section, list all of the family and personal treasures you would put in a time capsule to be opened in the year 2100 and explain your choices. If you or your family has a box, chest, or drawer of special items, list what you remember seeing there and give your impression of each item.

Journal Assignment 4   In your Commonplace Book, make a list of your favorite books since childhood. Make another list of books you would like to read someday. Make yet another list of your favorite movies and another list of favorite bands and CDs. Finally, write down something—a quote, a lyric, a scene, or a story—from a book, movie, or CD that means something to you.

Journal Assignment 5   In your Working Journal, tell the story of an event that recently occurred and was reported in the news. Make sure your retelling is at least eight sentences long and does not leave out any important information. If you can't think of a recent story, watch the news or read a newspaper to find one. When you are finished, go back over your work and make certain that you have adequately summarized the event.

Journal Assignment 6   In your Personal Diary, talk about the events of yesterday, trying not to forget anything. When you have finished, rewrite your entry on the following page while adding more details to make the events more vivid.

Journal Assignment 7   In your Working Journal, retell a story you think other people would enjoy hearing that has been told in your family for years and that you have probably heard a hundred times. For fun, if you have often heard this story from one particular person, you may want to try to tell it in his or her voice, exactly the way you have always heard it. When you have finished, double-check your work to be sure that you haven't left any important information out.

Journal Assignment 8   Cut out a magazine or newspaper picture, or find a dispensable photo, and affix it to one of two blank facing pages in your Commonplace Book. Explain what you think is going on in the picture. What happened just before the picture was taken? What happened afterward? If people seem to be talking in the picture, write down what you think they may be saying. Next, describe the picture as you would to someone who hasn't had and will never have the opportunity to see it. Write about the colors, the objects, the people in detail so that the person reading will get a precise mental image of the photo.

Journal Assignment 9   In your Working Journal, practice focused freewriting by sitting in a room of your home and describing everything in the room exactly as it looks to you from your perspective.

Journal Assignment 10   In your Commonplace Book, make a page of plans for your next twenty-five years. What would you like to be doing? Where would you like to live? What exotic places would you like to see on vacation or other travels? Would you like to learn any new languages, volunteer for any nonprofit organizations, take up some new hobbies? When you have finished writing out your plans, spend some time explaining how you will accomplish these goals.

Journal Assignment 11   In your Working Journal, affix a photo of a person from the newspaper, a magazine, or your personal albums. First, describe the person with words of positive connotation, making him or her as appealing and attractive as possible. Next, write a description of the same person using words with negative import, making him or her seem undesirable.

Journal Assignment 12   The decline of American culture seems to be a popular topic both in conversation and in the media these days. Write half a page in your Working Journal about your thoughts on the way culture is changing, if at all. When you have finished, return to what you have written and write one sentence that seems to express what you feel about the subject.

Journal Assignment 13   In your Working Journal, write "My Earliest Memories." Beneath this, list everything you can remember from early childhood, using as much specific detail as possible.

Journal Assignment 14   Go to your Class Notes section, and look over the notes you have taken so far this term. Are they adequate for helping you study for an exam? Then go to the Working Journal and write a paragraph analyzing your note-taking skills. Note the strengths and weaknesses. How do you plan to improve the weaknesses?

Journal Assignment 15   Go to a place where you may sit without being disturbed for twenty minutes. In your Working Journal, make extensive and accurate notes of the information coming to you from each of your five senses: sights, sounds, textures, light quality, mood, smells, temperature, and so on. You may even wish to make a sketch of the location of the objects and people you are describing for later reference.

Journal Assignment 16   In your Personal Diary, write about your current or future occupation. Write about the positive aspects and the negative aspects of that work.

Journal Assignment 17   Choose a favorite family photo and sit down with your notebook and the photo under a good light source. Choose an invention strategy, and brainstorm on the thoughts, memories, and feelings the photo suggests to you.

When you have finished, write a paragraph addressing the following questions: 1.) What would a person outside your family think was happening in the photo? 2.) What do you know of what was really happening when the photo was taken? 3.) What are the major changes that have occurred to those in the photo since it was taken?

Journal Assignment 18   In your Working Journal, describe someone you know very well from head to toe—literally start at the top of his or her head and end with his or her feet. Try to make your description so clear that someone who has never met him or her but has read the description would be able to identify him or her in a room full of people.

Journal Assignment 19   Many writers have been known to speculate about the ways in which the world will change on the day they die and what sort of day it will be—sunny with high humidity, rainy with earthquakes? These speculations range from the morbid to the humorous. Why not try the same—speculate on what kind of day the day of your death will be. Use plenty of examples to create the appropriate mood.

Journal Assignment 20   Poet Wallace Stevens wrote a poem entitled "Thirteen Ways of Looking at a Blackbird" in which he attempted to get closer to the idea of a blackbird by writing about it in every sense he could think of, some of them abstract and spiritual, some of them concrete. Think about an object, animal, person, or concept that is interesting and mysterious to you. Try to write down thirteen different ways your subject could be perceived. Be creative (don't avoid the weird—Wallace Stevens didn't), and number your perceptions.

Journal Assignment 21   Take time to think about events that have changed your life in some perceptible way. Think especially about occurrences that changed the way you thought or felt. Choose one of these events and, using an invention strategy, fill a page about what happened, who was there, why it was an important moment, and so forth.

Journal Assignment 22   Most of us have powerful memories of our high school careers. Take several minutes to think about the types of people with whom you attended school. Then write down four or five descriptive categories different people you recall would belong to. Once you have established the categories, go back to each and develop a definition of the category.

Journal Assignment 23   Think of your childhood. Using an invention strategy, write an answer to the following question: How did you survive the first ten years of your life? Think about the question from a serious standpoint, then think about it from a humorous point of view. Write briefly about each perspective.

Journal Assignment 24   Every action can be divided into many smaller actions. Think about your favorite activity—skiing, hiking, singing, playing soccer—and write about all of the processes associated with that action. Next, write about one specific memory when you were doing the activity. Use good, strong verbs.

Journal Assignment 25   Once in a while it is fun to feel nostalgic for "the old days" whether we mean our childhoods or just a few years ago. Think for a time about all the changes in technology and products in the last fifteen years. What are some of the products or objects you used to have that are no longer manufactured or are now obsolete? Write a comparison of then and now. Which do you like better?

Journal Assignment 26   How many times have you had an argument with yourself over something that you know you ought to do (or ought not to do) but that you don't want to do (or want to do anyway)? Think about a situation in which you may have to argue with yourself to get you to do something that is probably good for you in the long run. Write down the arguments you come up with.

Journal Assignment 27   Give yourself twenty minutes to write on the following topic: "The Internet: How It Has Changed Our Lives." Use invention strategies, define a topic, and make a quick outline. See how much of your outline you can complete before your time is up. How quickly were you able to focus your ideas? Write down a few insights about the way you work under pressure that you may have noticed from this exercise.

Journal Assignment 28   Think over the past term and remember the course of your progress. In what ways have you grown as a writer? As a student? What is your next step? What skills do you plan to continue working on? Write two pages in answer to these questions. Include any other issues that pertain to your personal growth.

Reading Skills

Capitalizing on the Reading-Writing Connection

There is perhaps no more important link to developing writing skills than being an enthusiastic reader. Recent studies show that average students' reading comprehension skills are declining. Instructors sometimes face classes in which there is not a single student who will admit to ever having read a book. It is not surprising, therefore, that instructors commonly struggle to help students whose reading and writing are both at levels far below the college standard. Every composition instructor struggles with finding ways to stress the importance of reading, knowing that there is little chance of becoming a good writer without it, but few of us are as successful as we would hope to be.

The Readings section in *The Writer's Workplace with Readings,* fourth edition, makes your job easier from the outset in several ways. Eclectic in style and subject matter, the essays have been sources of lively discussions in my classes. The authors of the readings originate from many cultures and socio-economic backgrounds, and, perhaps most importantly, possess a wide variety of viewpoints. Students are likely to find the selected readings both current and interesting.

The question remains: How does an instructor incorporate the readings in such a way that the students receive the most benefit out of the reading-writing connection?

Employing Reading Quiz Strategy

Few things can more easily derail a lesson than turning to an assigned reading, taking out your carefully prepared notes and questions, and embarking on the discussion only to be faced with the embarrassed silence that comes from few students having completed the reading assignment. Clearly, it is impossible for students to receive any benefits from reading if they are not, in fact, reading. Regular reading quizzes that will have some bearing on the students' final grades in the course are an easy method for providing reading incentive.

Avoid letting reading quizzes take much of your valuable classroom or grading time. Generally speaking, five questions will suffice. The students' answers should reflect more than surface comprehension, so a variety of types of questions often works well. Here is a quick example of a reading quiz over Tenaya Darlington's essay "Dream Houses."

1. *Vocabulary question*—What does "grandiose" mean?
2. *Test of reading*—Why do Darlington and her brother drive across town to sit in front of their old house?
3. *Reading Comprehension question*—How does Darlington feel about her parents' "dream house"?
4. *Reading Comprehension question*—What realization does Darlington come to in the essay about the definition of a "dream house"?
5. *Rhetoric question*—Describe some of the rhetorical techniques Darlington employs in the essay. (Narration, Description, Comparison)

It is a good idea to design the questions so that the answers will be short—no more than a sentence or two. If typing up quizzes and photocopying them prior to class is not possible, simply read through the questions twice slowly, and do not repeat for latecomers. You might want to further reduce your workload by having students exchange papers and grade one another's quizzes. Have students mark the number of correct answers clearly at the top of the page and have them pass the quizzes to you immediately. You may want to warn them that you do spot check the quizzes and keep them on file for the term to be reviewed if any question arises. If you dislike the concept of students grading one another's work (I find it a useful exercise in critical judgment), be sure to give the answers to the students verbally as soon as you have collected their quizzes.

Almost as important as the quiz itself is the incorporation of the quiz grades into the final course grade. Making class attendance, participation, and reading quiz grades a combined 10 percent of the final grade often provides adequate incentive for students to take the readings seriously. Some instructors make the quizzes themselves worth between 5 and 10 percent.

Leading Reading Discussions

When leading a class discussion on readings, instructors face several common difficulties: some students consistently speak out to the point of irritating other students and even squelching the discussion; other students, the "silent nodders," seem to want to participate but are perhaps intimidated; when discussing issues, students often seem to offer superficial statements of opinion rather than well-thought-out convictions; and they neither build on what other students have said nor seem to know how to constructively contradict an opposing view.

Consider the goals of a class discussion of a reading. Discussion should be the culmination of reading—we enjoy talking about what we have read in order to discover if other people have been moved in the same ways that we have. Discussion is also the test of reading comprehension—for we cannot hold a satisfactory discussion unless we have truly understood a reading. A good discussion also serves to fix the most important points of a reading in memory.

When leading the reading discussion, attempt to create a relaxed atmosphere without giving the impression that "anything goes." Consistently refer back to what students have previously said, mentioning them by name, restating their comments, and explaining how their ideas apply to where the discussion is heading. Show them that their words and ideas do have value and impact. Part of what you are helping them to learn through discussion is how to express themselves in a public situation, how to think and choose their words carefully to best express their thoughts. You may decide that having students sit in a circle so that they can address one another adds enough formality to be conducive to better conversations. Invite contrasting views from students and elucidate opposing viewpoints while maintaining a neutral position. Do not hesitate to ask a student who has spoken at some length to wind up his or her point so that another student can speak. Call on students who seem to have something to say but not the nerve to enter the conversation. When a student refers to or contradicts a point brought up by another student but addresses the comment to you, remind the speaker which member of the class originally mentioned the idea and encourage the speaker to address the comment to that person.

Another method incorporates small group discussions. Break the class into groups of three to five students each, and pose one or more thought-provoking questions for each group to answer by means of their discussion. When the groups are finished, one member from each group will report the answers they discussed, and the conversation can then continue on a higher level with the entire class involved.

Helping Students Who Do Not Read Well

We find a wide range of reading abilities in our developmental writing classrooms. The reasons for students who do not read well are equally varied.

Students who have a diagnosed learning disability need to be made aware during the first week of the term of all campus facilities and services available to aid them. Some campuses provide scribes and readers for students with learning disabilities and may further provide laptops for note taking while reading.

For students whose reading comprehension is weak, stress the benefits of reading aloud slowly and clearly to themselves when alone. It is sometimes the case that ill-prepared readers, in an effort to keep up with what they believe to be "normal" reading pace, read too quickly for their own comprehension. Reading aloud forces students to slow down to a conversational level. It also helps them understand the syntax of complex sentences because the voice places natural inflections on the phrasings that may not occur when they are reading silently to themselves. In addition, stress the importance of taking notes, looking up new vocabulary, asking questions, and underlining important passages.

Finally, for the uninterested reader, and for all readers for that matter, stress the importance of reading as an active conversation not a passive lecture. Make it an assignment for students to mark up one of the readings with underlines, highlighting, marginal notes, questions, and so forth. Walk around the room to see what their pages look like and hold up impressive examples so that the rest of the class can see. If students consistently complain that they did not like the readings, take that opportunity to discuss the source of their dissatisfaction. One of the "rules" I give to my students is that it is never enough to say, "I didn't like it," or "I thought it was boring." When I get a statement such as this in class, I ask the student to give me five specific reasons for his or her judgment. I help the student delve into the reasons by asking questions. A student who can state reasons for a particular response to a reading is developing critical skills for analyzing writing.

Incorporating Vocabulary Which Is Employed in Reading Classes

Many of our writing students are also enrolled in developmental reading courses. One simple way to stress the reading/writing connection is to use the same terminology that they hear in their reading classes.

I have had the great fortune to teach writing as part of a reading/writing/math/Freshman Experience block for several years. In our format, the students have combined reading and writing for one class period Monday through Friday for sixteen weeks. With two additional required hours of lab work, the students receive seven credits if they successfully pass the course. The reading instructor and I are in the classroom at the same time, which naturally reinforces the reading/writing connection for our students. To prevent confusing our students, I have learned to employ the same vocabulary as my colleague. Now, I refer to the topic sentence or thesis as the main idea, supporting details as major or minor details, and so forth. I constantly stress that there is little difference in the roles of reader and writer. As a reader, one previews an essay; predicts the topic and main idea; reads the work in question; revises the predicted main idea; rereads; and analyzes the work in terms of content, structure, and style. As a writer, one prewrites on a given topic; creates an initial topic sentence or thesis statement; uses invention strategies to develop it; writes a rough draft; revises the topic sentence or thesis; edits for unity, coherence, and structure; and, finally, proofreads for errors and stylistic opportunities to create the final draft. Whether serving in the role of reader or writer, a student must ask many of the same critical questions. The student writer at some point in the writing process must imagine himself or herself to be a reader in order to clearly communicate. Our results in students' reading and writing improvement by employing this method have been exceptional.

Reading Activities for *The Writer's Workplace with Readings,* Fourth Edition

Reading Activity 1   "Summer Reading" by Michael Dorris. There are five sentence fragments in Dorris's essay. Find all of them, then turn each into a complete sentence.

Reading Activity 2   "Summer Reading" by Michael Dorris. Find five examples of sentences that used coordination to join more than one idea. Write each sentence over as a sentence joined by subordination. Read Dorris's sentences and your own version again and decide which you think sounds better and why.

Reading Activity 3   "My Daughter Smokes" by Alice Walker. Because we experience events in time sequence, most stories follow chronological order and are said to have a beginning, a middle, and an end. However, in Walker's essay, the author chooses different moments from her life and her father's and sister's lives, some of them in sequence but all with large stretches of time between them, to tell her story. Plot out a time line of the different moments of her story on a separate sheet of paper with a brief note about what occurs each time. Why do you think Alice Walker chose to tell her story in this way?

Reading Activity 4   "My Daughter Smokes" by Alice Walker. Walker tells her story in a series of anecdotes. Reread her essay and mark the anecdotes that you find the most effective. Are there any that surprise you? Next, take time to think over moments of your life that could be anecdotal and jot down three stories (they are probably stories that you have often told in the past) that you think express important qualities about your character or the forces that have shaped you.

Reading Activity 5   "The Paterson Public Library" by Judith Ortiz Cofer. Because we experience events in time sequence, most descriptions are told in chronological order. In Ortiz Cofer's essay, the author chooses to describe events and places both in chronological order and spatial order. What do the different descriptions add to Ortiz Cofer's overall thesis? Choose four descriptions and analyze the manner in which the details are organized.

Reading Activity 6   "The Paterson Public Library" by Judith Ortiz Cofer. Underline the subjects and circle each complete verb in paragraphs 1–3. Highlight the topic sentence in each paragraph. If you cannot detect a topic sentence, jot down the controlling idea in the margin next to the paragraph.

Reading Activity 7   "Sleepless in El Paso" by Leo N. Miletich. Find ten irregular verbs in the essay. Write down the present infinitive, and present and past participle of each.

Reading Activity 8   "Sleepless in El Paso" by Leo N. Miletich. Find the words or phrases with negative connotations in the descriptions Miletich uses. In each case, change the word or phrase to one of neutral or positive connotation.

Reading Activity 9   "Sticky Stuff" by Kendall Hamilton and Tessa Namuth. Hamilton and Namuth give a definition of "entropy" in the first paragraph. Paraphrase the definition (look it up in the dictionary if you need to). Next, give three to five examples of entropy that you have personally experienced.

Reading Activity 10   "Sticky Stuff" by Kendall Hamilton and Tessa Namuth. There is a sentence fragment in Hamilton and Namuth's first paragraph. Locate the fragment; then decide if their use of the fragment is effective (a so-called "good fragment") or distracting. Argue your opinion for or against.

Reading Activity 11   "Freewriting" by Peter Elbow. Look at the example of freewriting that Elbow uses for illustration. Rewrite the passage, correcting all errors in grammar and usage. How many did you find?

Reading Activity 12   "Freewriting" by Peter Elbow. Summarize the main points of Elbow's essay systematically, paragraph by paragraph. Rewrite your summary in standard summary format.

Reading Activity 13   "Neat People vs. Sloppy People" by Suzanne Britt. Underline examples of good supporting detail in Britt's essay. Does Britt use better details in describing the habits of neat people or sloppy people? Explain the difference— why do you suppose the author made those choices?

Reading Activity 14   "Neat People vs. Sloppy People" by Suzanne Britt. Underline the transitional words and phrases Britt uses. Do you think she has enough? Too many? In paragraphs 6 through 12, put a double line under the topic sentence or jot down the controlling idea in the margin.

Reading Activity 15   "Dream Houses" by Tenaya Darlington. Outline Darlington's essay, paragraph by paragraph. Does she employ a block format or a point-by-point format for her comparison/contrast? Decide whether the other format would have been more effective for her essay, and explain your answer.

Reading Activity 16   "Dream Houses" by Tenaya Darlington. Identify the metaphors and similes Darlington uses throughout the essay. In each case, determine whether a flat description would have been as effective. Finally, in a paragraph, using Darlington's metaphors and similes as examples, write an explanation of the purpose of using these devices in descriptive writing.

Reading Activity 17   "Requiem for the Champ" by June Jordan. Often it is difficult to get a handle on the difference between cause and effect. Scan the reading and decide whether it deals with causes or effects or both. Explain your answers in writing.

Reading Activity 18   "Requiem for the Champ" by June Jordan. Mark each occurrence in which the author employs an example, extended example, illustration, or anecdote. When you finish, go back and try to identify which of the four types of example you have discovered.

Reading Activity 19   "TV Addiction" by Marie Winn. List the arguments that Winn makes to prove that television is addictive. Create a list of possible counterarguments. How convincing are Winn's arguments to you? Explain your answer.

Reading Activity 20   "TV Addiction" by Marie Winn. Using Winn's definition of drug or alcohol addiction, explore the possibility that there may be a newer phenomenon known as "Internet addiction."

Reading Activity 21   "The Truth About Lying" by Judith Viorst. Analyze the effectiveness of Viorst's use of the second-person point of view (she addresses the reader as "you"). Why did she choose to direct questions to the reader? Do you agree with her decision?

Reading Activity 22   "The Truth About Lying" by Judith Viorst. Come up with three more categories of lies that Viorst did not include, and create a definition for and give three examples of each.

Reading Activity 23   "The Changing American Family" by Alvin and Heidi Toffler. In paragraphs 1, 9, 10, and 17 explain the reason for each capitalization that does not occur at the beginning of a sentence.

Reading Activity 24   "The Changing American Family" by Alvin and Heidi Toffler. Underline the transitional words and phrases the authors use. Draw a double line under the subjects and verbs in paragraphs 1–4 and label each as either singular or plural.

Reading Activity 25   "Online but not Antisocial" by Janna Malamud Smith. Create an argument in opposition to Smith's, claiming in effect that the Internet is causing antisocial behavior (even if you agree with her position).

Reading Activity 26   "Online but not Antisocial" by Janna Malamud Smith. Analyze Smith's introduction. Does it spark your interest? Why or why not? What are the most interesting sentences in the introduction?

Reading Activity 27   "The Issue Isn't Sex, It's Violence" by Caryl Rivers. Carefully go through the persuasive essay and underline instances of supporting evidence. List the arguments Rivers makes, and then decide if you feel those arguments are strong. Can you think of other arguments for and against the author's position?

Reading Activity 28   "The Issue Isn't Sex, It's Violence" by Caryl Rivers. Make a list of all the details Rivers gives to create a causal link between rock lyrics and violence against women. Do you agree with her claim? Write a causal link which involves some type of music as the catalyst.

Reading Activity 29   "Unacceptable Behavior" by Lynda Chavez. Chavez uses strong language (also known as "emotionally loaded" language) throughout her essay. Find as many examples of strong language as you can. Substitute a neutral word or phrase for each example. How does that change the effectiveness of her argument?

Reading Activity 30   "Unacceptable Behavior" by Lynda Chavez. Set a timer to go off in one hour after rereading Chavez's essay so that it is fresh in your mind. Write a persuasive essay, arguing either for or against laws which make divorce more difficult. Use Chavez's essay for either support or to frame the opposing view. Stop writing when the hour is up.

Additional Reading Activities

There are many opportunities for introducing reading in the classroom. With a little creativity, you will find many accessible sources of useful exercise material. The goal should always be to pick writing sources which help students become more attuned to styles of language and persuasive techniques:

1. Have students bring in newspaper letters to the editor which they disagree with and have them write a response. You may wish to keep a number of letters to the editor on file to ensure the success of this exercise as students invariably forget their articles or are not pleased with the letters they find in the paper.

2. Tell students to bring in a paragraph of writing which they feel is very well written and another that they feel is poorly written. Have the students read their choices aloud and help them discuss the relative strengths and weaknesses of each. The advantage of this exercise is that it develops students' vocabulary for discussing and analyzing written works.

3. Give students advertisements with a substantial amount of copy and have them evaluate the persuasive effects of both the text and the visual. Then have them analyze the ways in which the two interact.

4. Hand out a difficult passage of writing—a poem, a paragraph of technical or legal jargon, or a paragraph that was written more than 50 years ago—and have students analyze it and paraphrase it in groups. Be sure to have a good dictionary and thesaurus on hand.

5. Have students bring in five one-page samples of junk mail they have received, or keep a paper sack handy when you go through your own mail so that you will have authentic examples to use (black out your address!). In pairs, have students analyze the persuasive techniques used by the authors of the letters.

6. Have students write summaries of two articles from newspapers or magazines, paying close attention to summary form.

7. Ask students to bring in several old letters or hard copies of e-mails they have received (the shorter the better). Have them analyze the writing in the letters and the stylistic choices the author made. Have them rewrite the letter for clarity, improved tone, correct grammar and usage, style and/or tone; then, assign the students to write a response to one of their classmates' letters.

8. Teach the students how to download free e-books onto their hard drives or disks. You may wish to assign part of an e-book as a supplemental reading assignment.

Group Exercises in Reading

The following are several group exercises designed to promote healthy class discussions of readings:

1. Every week assign one reading to a four- to five-student panel with the instructions to prepare a 10-minute presentation on a reading. It may

be an essay from *The Writer's Workplace,* a current article from a newspaper or magazine, or a chapter from their textbook. Ask the panels to be sure to define difficult vocabulary, analyze essay structure, give examples of style, and discuss argumentative techniques. They should clearly point out details, themes, and main points. Have each panel "lead" the discussion with the rest of the class, being sure to ask the rest of the class pertinent questions.

2. Have students choose one passage out of the assigned reading which seems the most interesting and meaningful to them; then, have them freewrite in their journals about that passage for ten minutes. Discuss some to the students' writings at the beginning of the discussion. The students will immediately be more focused and have a basis for more thoughtful commentary.

3. Give students a similar topic to the one in the assigned reading; and, after taking time to talk about the stylistic personality of the writing, have them attempt an imitation. By working on a conscious imitation, students will think deeply about sentence structure, tone, mood, and audience.

4. Have students write in their journals on a topic or question related to the reading assignment for ten minutes before beginning a discussion. This is particularly helpful when the reading concerns a controversial issue as it helps them surpass their initial superficial responses in favor of deeper concerns.

Study Skills

What Are Study Skills and How Can They Be Taught?

It is a rare student who does not need to improve his or her study skills to some extent. But when we speak of study skills, exactly which skills do we mean? On the most basic level, students should have the goal of being able to recall what they read with accuracy, analyze the import of their reading clearly and critically, and summarize the main points of their studies in written form. Students must be aware of the resources available to them when they do not understand crucial points in their studies, and they must be capable of using them. But, perhaps most important, they need to develop an active study attitude—looking up words that are unfamiliar to them, going to the library or home resource books to answer questions, and keeping helpful, accurate notes of their class time.

Identifying the need for these skills is far easier than teaching the skills themselves. Clearly impress upon the students the importance of these skills several times during the term, provide them with advice and study skills activities, and hope that they begin to see the benefits in their work for themselves.

Why Emphasize Good Study Skills?

Ultimately, our goal as writing instructors is to produce not just people who are clear writers and competent readers but also people who are critical thinkers. It is through the act of writing that we discover what we really think about a topic or issue. The organizing agent of verbalizing brings forth ideas and connections that were previously buried. Moreover, reading carefully and with interest is one of the best spurs to writing well; interacting with an author's ideas and then comparing and contrasting our thoughts and values with someone else's helps us discover the direction to take our own writing.

Students beginning their college careers at the precollege level often have difficulty with all of these fundamentals. Some come from deficient academic backgrounds, others lack the family superstructure to immediately comprehend the demands of higher education (they may be the first in their families, and even in their acquaintance, to pursue a college degree), and others may have acquired the attitude that they are passive members of the learning process, and that the active role belongs to the instructor alone. Whatever strides you make with them early on in these study areas will ensure success in the course and all parts of their future education. You may find that they will benefit by spending time on listening skills in the beginning to encourage accurate, helpful note taking. Working steadily and patiently on reading skills will yield results in all of the other areas. Remember that the overriding goal is for students to be able to understand and synthesize ideas and information.

The Importance to Your Students of Having a Clean, Well-Lighted Place

Although this next issue may seem too basic to mention, you may be surprised, upon taking a casual poll, how few of your students have desks or designated study areas at home. In keeping with the theme of *The Writer's Workplace* title, take some time to cover the basics of a good reading/writing/study area. Have students write about the place or places they normally go to study and how long they spend there. Discuss such issues as listening to music or television while studying and allowing interruptions from telephone calls, children, and other family members.

Next talk about what makes a study area a good place to work. Ask what kinds of materials are important to have at hand and what types of resources they find indispensable. Here is a possible list you may use as the basis for the advice you will give the students:

Important qualities of a work area: Quiet with the option of soft music, a good light source, uncluttered, not overly comfortable (e.g., overstuffed chair or bed).

Materials to have on hand: Plenty of paper (both notebook paper and typing paper), Post-It notes, word processor or computer, lots of pens and pencils (and a dependable sharpener), a stapler with standard staples, highlighter pens, paper clips, scissors, tape, manila envelopes, and folders.

A List of Helpful Home Resources:

- A good college dictionary, such as *Webster's New Collegiate Dictionary* (Merriam Webster),
- a pocket dictionary (for looking up spelling quickly),
- an unabridged thesaurus, such as *Roget's International Thesaurus,*
- the most recent world almanac, for recent statistics on important issues,
- a desk atlas, such as Rand McNally *Country Atlas,*
- a desk encyclopedia, such as *The Concise Columbia Encyclopedia,* Judith S. Levy and Agnes Greenhall, eds., or *Encarta* or other encyclopedia software,

- a dictionary of literary characters, literary terms, authors, and basic plots, such as *Benet's Reader's Encyclopedia,*
- a book of concise world history, such as *The Timetables of History* by Bernard Grun (Simon and Schuster),
- a book of quotations, such as *Bartlett's Familiar Quotations* (Bartlett's can also be found on the Internet),
- a book on the finer points of writing style, such as *The Careful Writer* by Theodore M. Bernstein (Atheneum) or *The Elements of Style* by William Strunk and E.B. White (also available on the Internet at Bartleby.com),
- and, of course, favorite books.

Explain the benefits of each of the items on the list you choose, then follow up by having the students write about the deficiencies in their own work areas and how they plan to correct the situation. Be sure to discuss their answers.

You might consider assigning a journal exercise (for either in-class or out-of-class work) that has students imagine their idea of the perfect study space. Some might want lots of windows looking out over beautiful gardens, others a wood paneled library, redolent of leather chairs and old paper. Invariably, students write about the calming effect of burning a candle. No matter what they come up with, the exercise helps reinforce the idea that studying, reading, and writing are such important activities that they deserve to have a place designated for performing them. This assignment also provides good practice in description.

How to Integrate Study Skills Into the Curriculum

Within the first week, have students make a contract with themselves called the Study Plan Pact. Before creating this contract students should be fully aware of all of the many demands that the course will make on their time: grammar, usage, and structures exercises; readings and activities; journal writing assignments; home writing assignments; and exams. Have the students devise a personal plan of action for the semester—what time of day will they study? Where will their studying usually take place? How much time will they spend studying per day (you might remind them that the rule of thumb is one or two hours of study/work time for every hour spent in class). Students should also list large demands on their time—other very difficult courses they are taking, employment, children, etc. They should not be allowed to submit the contract without offering at least three suggestions for solving the conflict between study time and these other demands. When students have finished the plan, one copy should be handed in to you to be kept on file, and another copy should be stapled to the inside front cover of their notebooks.

Instructors would be wise to give students a brief assignment early in the term which requires them to find the campus library and locate some basic information there. Some campuses have a regularly scheduled library tour for composition students, and if your campus is one of these, take every advantage of the library staff's cooperation by having students explore all of the different sections, including audio visual rooms, study rooms and carrels, computer facilities, on-line and regular card catalogues, and CD catalogues and Internet access. Students need to know the resources available to them as soon as possible even if they do not discover a need for the resources until much later.

During the term, you will check students' journals periodically. Take this opportunity to look at the quality of the class notes they are keeping. You will be looking for a happy medium between mere verbatim notes from the board and your lectures and an unhelpful, disjointed scrawl of a few notes here and there. Ideally you will want to find accurate notes combined with synthesis notes in the student's own writing—comments on what a particular term means or how the newer information builds on what has come before. The standard is whether you deem the notes to be helpful for preparing for some other activity such as a midterm or final exam. You may wish to grade this section of the journal according to the standards you have agreed on with the class in order to reinforce the importance of their note-taking skills. As an exercise, you could try one or both of the following two methods to encourage accurate note taking: At the beginning of the next class period following a lecture or assigned reading, give a quiz over the material covered but allow students to use their notes to answer the questions. Before you give a lecture, tell your students that you will administer a quiz over the material you are about to cover and that they will be allowed to use their notes as they take the quiz. I have had excellent results with both methods.

Another way to integrate study skills is to spot check their textbooks from time to time for signs of active reading—underlined or highlighted passages, notes and questions jotted in the margin, and so on. Show them examples of books you have read and marked up. An authentic example is far more persuasive than a textbook mock-up of active reading notes. If the students' textbooks are relatively free of marks of any kind (perhaps because they are hoping to sell the book back to the college bookstore or because they feel uncomfortable writing in books as a rule), either remind them that *The Writer's Workplace with Readings* is a consumable workbook that cannot be resold or have them show you the notes they have written in their journals which correspond to a given reading. If there are no notes or the notes are both sloppy and unhelpful, make it clear that they need to do more conscientious work. You may wish to give deductions to students who consistently show little effort in this area.

Study Skills Activities

1. One of the most important study skills activities you can use with your students is testing their reading comprehension by having them do summaries of essays. Basic summary form dictates that the author's name and title of the work are mentioned at the beginning of the summary and that the main points of the essay are contained in the summary in the order that they are mentioned in the original. Such a simple format gives students a means for guiding their thoughts; what you should look for, however, is whether or not students have comprehended the thrust of the essay and whether they have understood its thesis and tone. Try a three-part summary exercise using three short pieces, each more complex than the last. I have had good luck with photocopying a summary from each student (after removing names) and handing out a packet of summary examples to each member of the class. Reading the summaries is actually a home reading assignment with the added task of making note of any part of a given summary which is either 1.) too close to the wording of the original, 2.) misrepresents the original, or 3.) is an addition to the original. When we come back together the following class period, we analyze the summaries one by one, noting strengths and a few weaknesses.

2. This activity combines both reading and note-taking skills: at some point mid-semester, have students turn to the back of their journals to where they keep a running vocabulary list gleaned from the readings. Give them ten to fifteen minutes to review their lists. Then, give a vocabulary quiz using any difficult vocabulary from the readings you have already covered. The idea is that students who have been keeping careful notes of words they need to learn should be able to refamiliarize themselves with the definitions in ten to fifteen minutes in order to do well on the quiz, whereas students who have kept few notes will probably not be able to recall the definitions when needed unless the words are already a part of their working vocabularies. This quiz makes a clear point as to whether or not you decide to record the grades; however, if you try this exercise more than once, grade the subsequent quizzes.

3. At the end of a unit when there is a little time left over, select two readings between three and five paragraphs in length that have complex messages. Divide the class in half, and give a different reading to each half. Tell them to take very good notes on the readings because you will be giving them a quiz over the material at the end of twenty minutes. When students have finished taking notes, have them exchange notes with a member of the other group and collect the readings. Give a short quiz to each group on the essay they did not take notes for. Tell them that they must use the notes given to them to answer the questions. When the exercise is completed, read each essay aloud—there will usually be a lot of laughter as students realize how misled they were by the notes they were using to take the quiz. Talk about the importance of accurate note taking. The students will readily agree.

4. When reviewing for an exam, have students work in groups to compare notes that they have taken over the course of the term. Allow students time to copy missing notes and discuss confusion over some of the material that they may not feel comfortable voicing in front of the whole class. The point of this exercise from your standpoint is that, although students should be doing this type of work out of class and on their own time, stronger students have probably found one another early in the term and are sharing ideas and information out of class whereas weaker students are probably not. This gives a structured background for the weaker student to supplement his or her notes with valuable material while finding out exactly how the stronger student works and takes notes.

5. They've heard about interactive computer programs. Now talk to students about interactive reading. Stress to them that reading is much more like having a conversation than watching a television program. When you are participating in a good conversation, you normally ask questions. The same is true of a good reading. Tell them to ask the reading—or more exactly the author of the reading—questions about issues they want answers to. By anticipating the author's response, students stand a better chance of comprehending when the author does finally address a given issue.

For an exercise, lead the class through a short reading from the book, stopping every second paragraph and asking the class, "What do you think the author is leading up to? What do you want to know next?" Write their questions on the board and check them off as they are answered as you continue to read. Explain that they will perform the whole process mentally after a while.

6. Give students an opportunity to explore different resources either in their home resource library or the college or local library. Provide a list of questions for them to answer. Tell the students that they will be required to report the source where they found the answer (to avoid their merely asking someone who might know). Your list of questions might look something like this:

1. What is the current estimated population of China?

2. Name ten species that are currently endangered.

3. Give five synonyms of the word *politician.*

4. What is the root of the word *cyclone*?

5. What is the plot of *White Noise* by Don Delillo?

6. What happened in history and politics between 1300 and 1350 AD?

7. Which U.S. city has the highest per capita income?

8. Who won the 1999 Pulitzer Prize?

9. Who was Zora Neal Hurston?

10. What is the total land area of Africa?

If students balk at the difficulty of questions such as these, assure them that the answers are readily available if they choose the right source. To prove your point, bring in three or four sources and another list of questions. Ask for volunteers and have them try finding the answers in the available sources.

Chapter 1   An Invitation to Writing

Whether they are fully aware of it or not, students are about to embark on an exciting journey to find the writer inside themselves. *The Writer's Workplace* begins with an in-depth discussion of professional writers' primary tool—a journal notebook. Because the journal is such a crucial element in the development of ideas, carefully go through each of the activities in the chapter and have students transcribe their answers in their Working Journal as their first home journal assignment.

It is very important at this stage that students feel encouraged to ask questions and offer opinions. Here are some possible activities to get things rolling:

1. Bring in selections from famous writers' diaries and journals (either copy for all of the students or read aloud). After reading the journal entry, read a paragraph or so of something they have written. Good examples for this would be Virginia Woolf's diaries and a selection from *To the Lighthouse;* or John Cheever's diaries and the ending to his short story, "The Swimmer." Other famous diarists include Anais Nin, Sei Shonagon (*The Pillow Book*), Samuel Pepys, and Benjamin Franklin.

2. Show students the process of writing from journal to finished essay, story, or poem. For this exercise, you may wish to bring in some of your own journal work to share with the class; or you may have student examples on file that you have received permission to use; or you could locate *The Poet's Notebook: Excerpts from the Notebooks of 26 American Poets* edited by Stephen Kuusisto et al. (Norton, 1995). No matter which examples you decide to use, students will surely appreciate actual examples of the journal in action.

Chapter 2   The Elements of Good Writing

Students often confuse the terms "unity" and "coherence." For an exercise in coherence, have students underline every logical connector or transitional word or phrase in several paragraphs from the reading section of the text. Have the same paragraphs already enlarged and copied to a transparency master, and, using a black marker, mark out each of these they find. Ask them what they think is lost by deleting these words. Often, they will easily get the point. For unity, draw a large umbrella on the board or transparency. Within the umbrella, write a topic sentence such as "Stress can cause many problems in a student's life." Tell them that only people who belong to that topic sentence can stand under the umbrella, and then give them supporting details, one at a time, and ask if they belong under the umbrella or outside (in the rain). This is just one quick visual device to help them relate "umbrella" with "unity."

Chapter 3   Finding Subjects and Verbs in Simple Sentences

By laying a strong foundation with subjects and verbs, *The Writer's Workplace* helps students increase their chances of success with future sentence work. Without the ability to locate the subject and verb in every sentence they encounter, students cannot possibly comprehend major usage errors such as run-ons and fragments. Therefore, Chapter 3 provides a wide range of activities in locating subjects: in simple sentences, sentences with prepositional phrases, sentences that begin with expletives *here* and *there*, sentences with understood "you," and sentences that contain appositives. In addition, the chapter covers finding verbs—action verbs, linking verbs, and helping verbs. The chapter concludes by helping students identify the parts of speech.

Given the nature of the material and the timing within the term, you may wish to take this opportunity to ease tensions and help the class jell by playing a two-team identification game. Divide the board in half and list all of the parts of speech on each half. Choose any reading from the textbook, toss a coin to see which team goes first, and the winning team must find the subject and verb of the first sentence of the chosen reading. If their answer is incorrect, the question goes to the other team. If neither team gets the answer correct, the first team to correctly identify another part of speech within the same sentence receives a point. Then go on to the next sentence until ten sentences or twenty minutes have expired—whichever comes first. The winning team will be asked to name every part of speech in the final sentence of the essay. Some prize!

Chapter 4   Making Subjects and Verbs Agree

This chapter covers subject-verb agreement on many levels. It discusses the problem of subject-verb agreement with pronouns, with verbs *do* and *be,* with hard-to-find and hidden subjects, with group nouns, with indefinite pronouns, with compound subjects, and with unusual nouns and plurals.

One of the common difficulties students face when working through this material is having to come to terms with their own dialectical idiosyncrasies—the standard English "she does" may sound overly formal, strange, or simply wrong to a speaker whose home dialect dictates "she do." As an instructor, be sensitive to these problems while remaining firm as far as the necessity that all students master the material. You might want to explain standard English by employing an analogy to so-called "business English." Both are ways of speaking and writing in professional and public arenas while everyone is free to maintain familiar dialects at home.

When devising exercises to accompany this section, remember that each exercise should employ the simple present tense since it is the only tense that forces the writer to pay attention to subject-verb agreement. Here are a few possible examples:

1. Bring in a 10-minute videotape of a sporting event. Have students practice being sports announcers giving a play-by-play account of the action. If the technology is not available for video, give directions to several students to mime a specific action while a panel of students gives a moment-to-moment account of what they are doing. Keep track of any mistakes that students make in subject-verb agreement and discuss these mistakes when the exercise is over.

2. Assign the class to visit a campus commons or community center. It is important that they witness many people doing different activities. Have students write for fifteen minutes about all of the activities they see in the present tense. Upon returning to class, have students exchange papers and look for subject-verb agreement errors.

3. Hand out a short piece of about two paragraphs in length which is written in the past tense. Put students in groups of twos or threes and have them rewrite the piece in the present tense without making mistakes in subject-verb agreement.

Chapter 5   Understanding Fragments and Phrases

Students who were encouraged to "write the way they talk" in order to help them overcome their fears of writing often have problems with sentence fragments since fragments are common in conversation. For example, a novel in which the characters always speak to one another in complete sentences seems stilted and unnatural. Chapter 5 addresses the issue of fragments pragmatically. Now that students have a good grasp of subjects and complete verbs, they are expected to identify incomplete sentences and correct them by supplying missing elements. The topic of fragments naturally leads to the subject of phrases and culminates in a lengthy explanation of the participle and participial phrase—one of the most common sources of fragments in student writing. The discussion of phrases sets the stage for discussion of more complex usage problems, namely run-on sentences.

Magazine advertisements abound in sentence fragments. There are several reasons for this—fragments can be emphatic, they stand out from sentences because they are unusual or even irritating, and they can create a conversational tone. Find an assortment of ads that contain fragments and give several ads to each group. Have the groups identify all of the fragments in the ads. Then change each fragment into a complete sentence. Next, have the group analyze the difference the complete sentences make on the overall tone of the ad. When the groups have had sufficient time to work, have them present their findings on one or two of the ads to the rest of the class.

Another exercise requires you to copy a short scene from a comedy that contains a number of fragments in the interchanges. Have students work in groups to make the fragments into sentences. Once this task is accomplished, assign roles for the original scene and roles for one of the revised "fragment-less" scenes. Have students read, or even perform, each version and then discuss the differences. What has happened to the comedic effect?

Chapter 6   Combining Sentences Using the Three Methods of Coordination

Students will be steadily encouraged to attempt more complex sentences as they proceed through *The Writer's Workplace.* The first step toward this goal will be taken in Chapter 6 as students learn ways to combine sentences through coordination. Students who tend to write short, choppy, primer-style sentences will benefit the most during this chapter, but all students will receive valuable training in using commas and coordinating conjunctions correctly, as well as semicolons and adverbial conjunctions.

At this stage you would do well to introduce several concepts that will become increasingly important as students gain writing confidence. First, not all short sentences should be joined using coordination—only sentences of equal importance and which contain related ideas. Encourage them to leave other types of short sentences alone for the time being. Second, the use of the appropriate coordinating conjunction is a crucial logical and meaningful link. Have students take special care to use the best conjunction and to avoid overuse of "and." Third, semicolons should be used sparingly—some students figure out early on that semicolons are the easiest answer to every coordination question and begin to overuse them; this becomes a hard habit to break!

A good exercise to use with the class is to provide groups with a list of short choppy sentences that pertain to the same topic. The groups must create a "paragraph" which sounds good and makes sense by combining the sentences appropriately. You may wish to specify that students use all of the methods of coordination at least once; or you may wish to hone their critical skills by leaving the choice up to their own discretion, and then ask them to articulate the reasons for their choices.

Chapter 7   Combining Sentences Using Subordination

One of the most difficult concepts for students to master is that of dependent and independent clauses, yet much of their future success hinges on the ability to distinguish between the two in a split second. Relative clauses cause even more problems than other types of dependent clauses because it is harder to detect the "mini-sentence" in them.

If you find students hitting the wall right away, review the parts of speech and all of the different types of phrases, showing the difference between an incomplete verb in a participial phrase and a complete verb in the clause. In some cases, you may have to review locating subjects and complete verbs as well. After students have worked through the exercises in the chapter, have them turn to a reading in the final section of the textbook. Choose one paragraph and as a class go through it slowly and identify dependent and independent clauses. When students have trouble, patiently help them identify and eliminate all of the prepositional phrases to get to the basic sentence. Give them the answer if they continue to be confused.

Probably the best way to learn dependent clauses is to compose them. Give students a list of short sentences that pertain to the same topic. Have them combine some of the sentences through coordination and others through subordination until they have a coherent "paragraph" that sounds good. Another tactic you may employ is to give students a relatively lengthy paragraph in which the majority of the sentences are joined through coordination. Have students read the paragraph to themselves, then aloud, and evaluate the writing style. When they decide that the author seems long-winded, have the students revise the paragraph by subordinating appropriate sentences.

Chapter 8   Correcting Fragments and Run-Ons

The Writer's Workplace simplifies the topic of run-ons by using it as a general term to describe "and" run-ons, fused sentences, and comma splices. Students commonly have difficulty distinguishing between the different types of usage errors, so this grouping will make your job easier by letting you stress the concept rather than the terminology. It may work well to review the basics of Chapter 6 on the three methods of coordination before beginning Chapter 8.

As you work through the chapter, take this opportunity to have students evaluate some of the writing assignments they have produced up to this point. After having students edit their own work for run-ons, have them exchange work and edit another student's work. If they have already eliminated the majority of errors in their home writing assignments, have them scour their journal assignments for errors.

Another exercise requires dictation. Tell students to write down the story you are about to tell them word for word. Proceed by telling a rambling story where most of your sentences are connected with "and." When you have told the story twice (exactly the same way both times), ask students to look over their dictation and eliminate run-ons by using the three methods of coordination and subordination. When they finish, have several read their finished products aloud.

Chapters 9 and 10   Making Sentence Parts Work Together

Students are ready to try their hands at fine-tuning in Chapter 9, which covers pronouns and case and pronoun-antecedent agreement, and Chapter 10, which deals with parallel structure and dangling modifiers. You will concentrate primarily on the work students perform on the many chapter exercises. If you have time, engage them on another level to break up the monotony.

Many students do not realize how important their mastery of the skills covered in Chapters 9 and 10 truly are, nor do they understand how mistakes in these areas mark a writer as inexperienced in both academic and business arenas. To stress the importance of the material, try some of the following:

1. Bring in newspaper headlines which have gross (and often funny) dangling modifiers.

2. Find dangling modifier bloopers in magazines (*Reader's Digest,* for example).

3. Create a confusing paragraph in which it is impossible to tell the antecedents of the pronouns (or find published examples).

This is another excellent opportunity to play an instructive grammar game. Divide the class into two groups. You may want to have the questions written on pieces of paper and placed in a paper bag. Have students come up one at a time and choose a question, which they write on the board so that the whole class can see it. Alternate teams and keep score.

Another activity also requires two teams. Each team composes the hardest test they can think of based on the parts of the chapter the class has covered (about 20 questions should be enough) and writes each question on a separate piece of paper and places them all in a bag. Students play the game again but this time they choose from the other team's bag. An alternative to the game would be for the students to compose the tests during one class period, whereupon you could take the tests to be copied and let the students take the opposing team's test the following class period.

Chapter 11   Practicing More with Verbs

It is hardly an overstatement to say that the key to fine writing is in the verbs, and good verbs begin with correct verbs. In Chapter 11, students will address all essential aspects of verbs: tenses, passive and active voices, and regular and irregular verbs. They will also learn to identify incorrect verb forms and shifts in verb tense.

Explaining the time sequence of complex verb tenses is a challenge for any instructor. Don't hesitate to map out sentences containing complicated sequences of tense on a time line. Have students come to the board and map out a sentence from the book. Reiterate the meaning of the various tenses, and show them how even complicated tenses show up in casual speech:

> "Yeah, I'll've been going to gymnastics classes for three years this September."
>
> "If that tire'd been flat, he'd've been in a world of hurt."
>
> "I've been reading the newspaper for the last hour."

Make it a goal to teach students to write all of the tenses of one regular and one irregular verb by the end of the unit.

Chapter 12   Using Correct Capitalization and Punctuation

This chapter covers ten basic rules for capitalization, eight rules for comma use, three uses for the apostrophe, four uses for quotation marks, three uses for the semicolon, four uses for the colon, and correct use of dashes, parentheses, and underlining/italics. Because you will be covering a great deal of material, you may wish to hand out study sheets (or copies of transparency masters) of the basic information you will be covering for students to follow along.

You will not need to spend much class time on capitalization after covering the ten rules, but you might try giving a spot quiz to see if the students are absorbing the material. You will need to spend time on rules for commas and uses for quotation marks. The information on semicolons will mostly be review from Chapter 6 on coordination.

Have students try the following exercise in groups once the chapter material has been covered:

> Tell a short, sad story of a man and woman who meet at the local Wal-Mart and fall instantly in love. Unfortunately, the man is buying a few items for his flight home to another state or a foreign country. They meet because the woman needs directions to the nearest medical center.

Tell students to pack the story with name brands, geographical locations, and dialogue. Have each group write a clean copy to submit for an activity grade.

Chapter 13   Choosing Words That Work

This first chapter of Part III introduces the students to the complex stylistic issue of word choice. As long as we are working within our own vernacular, we are all intensely attuned to the connotations and inflections of spoken and written speech. You may wish to exploit this fact if you find that students find the idea of connotation and word choice foreign. Write the following paragraph on the board or show it on the overhead projector:

> The small child turned the bowl of pasta over on the floor and sat down in it. Her mother was not happy about the child's action. After speaking loudly to the child, the father got something from the sink to help pick the pasta off the floor. The child spread the food across the floor and smiled.

Notice how many opportunities there are in the paragraph to give a negative connotation to the child's actions. Go through sentence by sentence and write better choices above the words and phrases that are weak or neutral. You may wish to provide another paragraph for students to work on individually or in groups.

Chapter 14   Paying Attention to Look-Alikes and Sound-Alikes

Even English instructors have trouble with *lay* and *lie* these days. Nevertheless, it is important for students to learn the difference between the many words that either look alike or sound alike. Some of the most pernicious problems students need work on are the differences between their/there/they're, to/too, then/than, and its/it's—to name just a few. Consider quizzing essential to making sure that students are soaking up the information.

Chapter 15   Review: Editing Student Writing

Students often learn more from peer examples than from professional writing examples because the former seem far more attainable. Your helping students to learn editing symbols at this point in their academic careers will make college-level English courses easier from the beginning. You may wish to embark on peer editing during this chapter by photocopying one of the weaker student papers and peer-editing handouts from the appendices, and spend half of a class period letting the students work in small groups answering the questions and marking the essay with symbols.

Chapter 16   Working with Paragraphs: Topic Sentences and Controlling Ideas

In this chapter you will be covering four basic but easily confusing concepts: What exactly is a paragraph? What is a topic sentence? Where is the topic in a topic sentence? How can you tell what the controlling idea of a topic sentence is? Students will also learn how to distinguish between a title and a topic sentence, which provides you with an opportunity to discuss sentence fragments and how to convert fragments—or titles—into complete sentences.

When presenting paragraph basics such as initial indentation, capitalization, ending punctuation, etc., do not neglect to mention that the block format is also quite common. However, the indented paragraph is still considered standard. This reinforces the students' understanding that the paragraph is more than five sentences joined on a page. You may discover that the most efficient way of teaching the paragraph is by examining what the paragraph is not.

Newspapers, especially letters to the editor sections, come in handy when talking about topic sentences. Show the class current headlines. Then have them convert the headlines into complete sentences. If the sentences do not yet contain a controlling idea, lead them through the steps needed to create one or more controlling ideas. Then have students identify the controlling ideas in headlines in letters to the editor. You may want to copy one good letter to be looked at by the entire class, having them identify the topic sentence in each paragraph.

Chapter 17   Working with Paragraphs: Supporting Details

Few of us complain about the overabundance of detail in students' essays. It is for that reason that the lesson on supporting details should be reinforced in a variety of ways. Chapter 16 helps students identify supporting detail and distinguish between the topic sentence and its supporting details. It also offers exercises to help them make supporting details specific.

The concept of supporting detail is rarely easy for students, but quite often several students in the class will realize breakthroughs in their writing when this concept suddenly becomes clear. You may first try to read a paragraph in which the language is decidedly vague. Beware: some students, probably under the spell of your oratory skill, will think the writing is good! Do not be overly critical of their tastes, but see if you can change their minds by reading the same paragraph again, but this time supplied with plenty of detail. Some will still like the first better, usually for an interesting reason—the vague version seems more spiritual, ephemeral, and prettier. Explain that one of the reasons they may like the vague version better is that nothing is concrete; therefore, all the details are supplied by the imagination of the readers and listeners. What they like is not the writing itself but their own imaginings based on the writing.

An excellent exercise at this stage is to take a vague paragraph and have students alone or in groups write the paragraph over by including lots of supporting details. This gives students the opportunity to incorporate everything they have learned in Chapter 16 with the newer information about supporting detail. A good way to wind up this exercise is to have groups of students read their paragraphs aloud so that everyone can hear all of the possibilities.

Chapter 18   Developing Paragraphs: Illustration

The illustration paragraph is the workhorse paragraph—it can be employed for many writing occasions. For students, it can also be considered the "training" paragraph. It gives them an opportunity to control their writing by recognizing the need for further examples to prove a given topic sentence.

Here is an illustration paragraph structure which employs reading curriculum terminology to get its point across:

- First Sentence: Make a claim about your topic that needs to be proven. (Topic Sentence or Main Idea)

- Second Sentence: Give one good reason that claim is true. (First Major Detail)

- Third Sentence: Give a specific example which explains or clarifies that reason. (Minor Detail supporting Major Detail)

- Fourth Sentence: Give another good reason that your claim is true. (Second Major Detail)
- Fifth Sentence: Give a specific example which explains or clarifies the second reason. (Minor Detail supporting Major Detail)
- Sixth Sentence: Give your last and best good reason that your claim is true. (Third Major Detail)
- Seventh Sentence: Give a specific example which explains or clarifies your last, best reason. (Minor Detail supporting Major Detail).
- Eighth Sentence: Write a neat, concluding statement summing up your position.

If you have your students use this chart several times, their writing will begin to sound better even to them. It is an excellent way to build their confidence before working with more complicated patterns.

Chapter 19   Developing Paragraphs: Narration

Students' favorite rhetorical form is often narration, but they would rather hear a good story than tell one. Storytelling at its best is a great deal more demanding than even impeccable describing; unfortunately, good storytellers make the job seem easy. This chapter will cover the most important aspects of narration: how to make a point with the narrative, how to arrange events chronologically, and how to use appropriate transitions.

In order to help the students understand what makes a good narrative, you may want to bring in short stories, or even short, short stories, to let students get a feel for what makes the narrative work (or fail). In addition, you may wish to take this opportunity to discuss direct and indirect quotation and the punctuation which accompanies each. A fun, and instructive, exercise along these lines is to bring in a tape of a dialogue (real people, not television) and have students transcribe the dialogue as closely to what they hear as possible. You will also want to discuss the difference between showing (scene work) and telling (exposition). You may even want to tell a lengthy joke and afterward have the students analyze the reason it is funny (or isn't).

A good place for students to begin their study of narrative is to tell a story of their own. There are several pitfalls even in this most natural of mediums. Because of proximity, students often describe family members in vague abstractions. Tell students to pretend that even family members are characters in a story they are creating and that it is all right to exaggerate and change the facts here and there for dramatic effect. Another common problem is that too often nothing happens in student stories—in fact, they are not stories at all but vignettes. This concept is more slippery—explain that *something must happen* in order to have a narrative. Therefore, having them choose their topic carefully with that in mind should alleviate most of the difficulties.

Chapter 20   Developing Paragraphs: Description

This chapter builds on Chapter 19 with an in-depth discussion of description. Students will learn to recognize and create a dominant impression through word choice and to identify and create sensory images. They will learn to order their description spatially and to write a descriptive paragraph step by step.

Many instructors notice that students enjoy the discussion of descriptive writing more than any other rhetorical pattern. Keeping this in mind, if you find that your class enjoys the section on description, try to bring descriptive exercises to class from time to time to help them further the skill. No other form of writing is quite as important for them to master because of its emotional appeal and versatility.

Take this opportunity to bring to class a varied selection of readings from novels, essays, and poetry. Monologues from plays that contain description can also work a nice contrast. For homework, the students could bring in a paragraph of description that they think is interesting.

A good exercise for beginning the unit is to have the students write for fifteen minutes at the beginning of class about the present moment—the chairs, people, marks on the board, quality of light, what can be seen from the window, etc. Tell them to write sharp, exacting detail. When they have finished, you may want to go over the details they noticed and to "sharpen" the images they have mentioned. When you cover spatial ordering, have students return to this exercise and revise spatially. When you finish the unit, have students rewrite the piece into a polished descriptive paragraph with a specific dominant impression.

Another exercise for either individual or group paragraph revision requires students to revise a neutral paragraph twice—first with a positive dominant impression and second with a negative dominant impression. Write or hand out a paragraph of description devoid of emotional content. Divide the board into two sections, each headed by a strong emotional word such as *fearful, comforting, warlike, jealous,* etc. The object is to create the mood of the description through word choice and imagery. The following is a simple paragraph example which can yield good results:

> While walking down a path, I came to a clearing. There was a small two-story house with four windows, a red door, and a chimney. In the backyard I could see a boat and a table. There were small animals and birds in the trees above.

Chapter 21   Developing Paragraphs: Process

When discussing process with students, it's a good idea to talk about the range in which it is used right from the start: writing recipes, giving advice on how to get the baby to sleep through the night, giving a scofflaw directions to the courthouse, giving commands for accomplishing an important project, to name just a few. In this chapter students will be given a working definition of process, they will have to identify whether or not a written process is complete, and they will learn to pay attention to logical sequence and to employ transitional words and phrases. At the end of the chapter they will be asked to write several types of process paragraphs based on models.

This pattern lends itself to myriad activities. A popular demonstration for process, which works particularly well in the ESL/EFL classroom, is the making of a peanut butter and jelly sandwich. You bring in the bread, the peanut butter, and jelly of your choice and set up a station at the front of the room. Have a volunteer give you commands for making the sandwich, which you then follow *exactly*. Students typically leave out a crucial step or two, or they are vague on important points such as "Put the bread together," the result being messy enough to require a few paper towels. Other possibilities are to bring in an appliance such as a coffeemaker and have students write directions for it. Students could also write down their favorite recipe but for an audience of eight-year-olds.

You might want to provide groups with a set of overly general directions to a common task and have them revise for unity and clarity. For a less advanced class, you can hand out several different hand-drawn maps and have groups compose a paragraph of directions from point A to point B. Have students with different maps exchange directions to see if they are clear enough for someone else to find his or her way.

Chapter 22   Developing Paragraphs: Comparison/Contrast

Students will address more complex structures in the Comparison/Contrast section. After a discussion of the basic principle behind the pattern, students will get practice in choosing and narrowing two-part topics before analyzing the differences in the point-by-point and block methods, and learning to recognize them in sample paragraphs. They will also learn about appropriate transitions and compose sample paragraphs step by step.

A challenging group exercise requires students to choose a two-part topic, narrow it, then brainstorm either similarities or differences between the subjects. Students then create one paragraph structured according to point-by-point and then two comparable paragraphs structured according to the block method using the same information.

The greatest difficulty you may face as an instructor in presenting this material is that students often choose to compare two topics with blatantly obvious similarities (vanilla bean ice cream and French vanilla ice cream) and contrast topics with readily obvious differences (living in the desert as opposed to living by the ocean). How do you impress on students that readers are interested in the surprising insight, the unusual take? In the following class exercise, students will be forced to use a combination of creative thinking and brainstorming to create more interesting comparisons and contrasts.

Write out several similar pairs and several dissimilar pairs:

Similar Topics

ice cream/frozen yogurt

bicycling/motorcycling

candlelight/cigarette lighter

movies/videos

Dissimilar Topics

ocean/desert

skateboarding/eating pizza

buying a house/having a baby

cutting your toenails/mowing the lawn

Start with a two-part topic that is similar, ice cream and frozen yogurt for example. Ask students to give you a list of the similarities: both are cold, both come in flavors, both can be found in the supermarket freezer. Take a two-part dissimilar topic—the ocean and the desert—and have students give you contrasting points: one is wet, the other is dry, one has sand on top and the other has sand on the bottom, one has cacti, the other has coral reefs, and so on. Ask students what they think of the prospects of an essay written on either topic. After a bit of prodding they will probably admit that the topics lend themselves to dull essays.

Next, try the opposite—what are the differences between movies and videos, two seemingly similar topics? Suddenly, the ideas begin to flow: when you watch a movie you feel as if you're a part of the action, but when you watch a video you can have a more intimate experience with the film because you're not responding as part of an audience.

Or try comparing buying a house to having a baby: both take about a year from start to finish; the rosy glow of pregnancy and deciding on a home may turn to fear and pain when delivery and closing costs occur; the feeling of satisfaction one has when walking into a house once the papers are signed and ownership is final, though it could never compare, may be the next best thing to holding your child in your arms for the first time.

Clearly, the point of the exercise is to show students that creativity often comes in surprising packages. Once you become good at orchestrating this exercise you may even have the students challenge you by trying to come up with a two-part topic that is so dissimilar they cannot imagine any similarities being drawn between the two. Prove them wrong—this is the perfect opportunity to discuss analogy!

Chapter 23   Developing Paragraphs: Cause and Effect

Students will learn to think more analytically about causal relationships in Chapter 23, which covers finding causes and effects in paragraphs, separating the cause from the effect, looking for the causal relationship, thinking about underlying and immediate causes and immediate and long-term effects, using transitions, and writing both cause and effect paragraphs step by step.

You will probably find that students have some trouble distinguishing cause from effect—it is no wonder since the effect of one event can become the cause of another event. In other words, you would do well to keep a broad view of causal relationships rather than attempt to simplify your explanation, which in this instance can serve to further confuse. Stress that when you discuss cause and/or effect it is relative to a specific issue or event. Also, you might mention that there are multitudes of causes so minute that they are impossible to label as such but they are every bit as real as the identifiable causes (think of Tolstoy's theory of the calculus of history in *War and Peace*), and are called influences. Effects are equally multitudinous, but it is easiest to identify those we can readily measure and see.

During your work on this unit, have students get into groups to analyze all of the many causes of a particular social issue. The groups should produce between twenty-five and forty causes. Then have the groups rank the causes in order of importance. Finally, they should decide which of these causes were immediate, underlying, and remote influences. When they have completed this assignment and the class has had a chance to compare notes, have the group work on the effects of the same issue. Students may wish to discuss whether defining causes or effects seems more truthful, or ask whether it is useful to talk about causes and effects. Open the floor for discussion concerning the persuasive import of this rhetorical pattern compared to what it adds to an author's style in terms of interest.

A list of intriguing cause-and-effect topics follows to help spark more topics if necessary. One of the best ways to build a cause or effect paper is by polling and/or interviewing people who can be used as supporting examples in the paragraph or essay. (See the appendix for handouts on "Conducting Surveys and Polls" and "Conducting Interviews" with a cause-and-effect focus.)

The causes or effects of drug abuse,

The causes or effects of child abuse,

The causes or effects of watching too much television,

The causes or effects of overpopulation,

The causes or effects of eating a high-cholesterol diet,

The effects of day care on young children,

The causes or effects of terrorism,

The effects of AIDS on social relationships,

The causes or effects of a Republican (or Democratic) Congress,

The causes or effects of prison overcrowding,

The causes or effects of exorbitant salaries in professional sports,

The causes or effects of airline ticket wars,

The effects of rapidly changing technology,

The effects of the Internet on modern lifestyles.

Chapter 24   Developing Paragraphs: Definition and Classification

When we are in the midst of a good argument on an issue, we constantly ask our opponents to "define your terms" and vice versa. Being able to clearly articulate a personal definition is an essential skill for the analytical thinker. Students will be asked to define words and concepts in this chapter in several ways: by classifying, by identifying characteristics, by giving examples, and by negation.

Have students bring their desk dictionaries to class. Ask them to find an interesting word and to write it down on a journal page along with its definitions. Talk a little bit about roots of words and have students study the roots of the words they have chosen. Then have them perform brainstorming clusters in several stages. First, tell them to brainstorm on all the personal associations they may have with the word and what it represents. Next, ask them to brainstorm on what the word is not. Then, have them brainstorm on classifications within this word and to list any characteristics that pertain to it. When they have completed these brainstorms, require them to write a paragraph which incorporates something from each of the different clusters. Have students read their definitions aloud.

For a critical thinking exercise, have students sit with their desks in a circle and present an issue to be discussed. Instruct the students to voice their opinions on the issue. Tell the students to listen very carefully to what the others are saying; if any statement seems vague, students should demand that the speaker define his or her terms. Take the discussion very slowly at first so that nothing is missed. When the conversation gets heated up, make notes of vague terms on a piece of paper and discuss the terms when the discussion concludes.

Chapter 25   Moving from the Paragraph to the Essay

In the opening discussion about essay writing, students are led through the entire writing process for producing the college essay: choosing a topic; distinguishing the controlling idea of a topic sentence; identifying and defining a thesis; brainstorming; selecting and organizing material; writing the rough draft; developing an idea in a paragraph; revising the rough draft for unity and coherence; editing the second draft; and preparing and proofreading the final copy.

It is a wise idea to focus on the first half of the process at this stage. Lead students through writing process activities that help them see the connection between topic and narrowed thesis. You may want to mention that brainstorming in search of a topic is as important as subsequent brainstorming since it generates interest in the writing task and eliminates common and mundane topics from the outset.

On the board write a general direction, "Write a description of a place." Have the class help you brainstorm using listing for a more interesting topic. Tell them you are going to throw out the first ten ideas the class has come up with—usually the best ideas are the last, whereas the first are quite basic and uninteresting. Choose the most promising topic of those left and write it on a fresh section of board.

Next, brainstorm on the chosen topic using clustering. You are now in search of an interesting thesis. Once again, eliminate between seven and ten of the ideas. Have students choose the most promising thesis from those remaining.

Finally, lead them through topic narrowing, using either listing or clustering. At this point, you may wish to require students to brainstorm individually and present their best ideas when they finish. Remind them to eliminate the first ten ideas and continue brainstorming for several minutes. If the exercise has gone well, the class should be left with five or so narrowed topics that are interesting enough to generate writing interest. You might want to mention that the process will eventually take a few minutes once they become accustomed to brainstorming.

Chapter 26   Watching a Student Essay Take Form

Chapter 26 reviews the material that was covered previously in Step One, but this time students observe the entire writing process in a single student essay from brainstorming, selecting and organizing material, writing the rough draft, revising for clarity of ideas to editing for correctness and preparing final copy.

Students may miss the importance of this chapter if you do not provide them with hands-on material to reinforce the stages of development. One suggestion is to find an example of student work from past semesters, which you have received permission to reproduce for classroom use, and which contains brainstorms, rough drafts, and a final draft. Copy the work and give it to the students in small groups.

Have students look first at the initial brainstorm and ask them to eliminate the weak topics and choose the strongest from among the ones listed in the brainstorm. Next, have students examine the second brainstorm for a thesis and choose the most interesting thesis from among those listed. Then, show students the brainstorm for topic narrowing and let them decide which narrowed topic seems most feasible. At this point, you may wish to have students work together to come up with a basic outline for the narrowed thesis before revealing the rough draft. When students examine the rough draft—you may want to read it aloud before they commence work—have them list all of the areas that should be reworked before the final copy. When you do show them the final copy, discuss the strengths and weaknesses of the paper and have them proofread it carefully.

If you do not have access to a student essay in all of the aforementioned stages, it is not too difficult to reconstruct the brainstorms to accompany a rough draft and final draft of a student essay. Allowing students to work through the whole process in this fashion, by allowing them to make choices, will prove to be an invaluable lesson in months to come.

Chapter 27   Writing an Essay Using Examples, Illustrations, or Anecdotes

Students will learn to distinguish between the types of illustrations that writers employ—whether from personal experience, hypothesis, research, or surveys. It is fair to say that most students will feel quite comfortable with examples from their own experience. Therefore, while not excluding that resource, it is important to expose them to the other types as painlessly as possible. Ideally, you might present a single issue and ask the class to provide support for it in each of the four ways. Afterward, ask students which types of illustration seem to be the most effective in proving the stance of the author. The firsthand experience, due to its compelling nature, almost always wins. However, if you ask which type of example *ought to be* the most persuasive, students will often say research. Use this as an excellent launching point for introducing a discussion about persuasion.

Another group exercise has students find statistics concerning a topical issue, such as incidence of cancer in the past year. Then students work together to create a paragraph built on statistical illustration. Encourage students to do a little library research on a particular topic. While they are in the library, you might assign them to find examples of all three types of illustrative techniques in published articles on their particular topic.

You may wish to have students conduct a minor survey at the mall, at work, or in their neighborhoods. They should take the task seriously and report their results in an illustrative paragraph.

Chapter 28   Writing an Essay Using Narration

Students will be required to expand the narration skills they have acquired in previous coursework. Important points for you to consider when helping them further their storytelling abilities are:

- Can students tell a narrative coherently with a beginning, a middle, and an end?

- Is there a point to the story they are telling? Does something happen or change?

- Do they supply enough supporting details to make the story seem real?
- Is there dialogue? Does it seem natural? Is it in the correct format?

Try the following as an exercise to hone these skills. Everyone has heard family stories that are so ingrained in their family lore that they could recite them from start to finish on request. Have the students write one of these stories. It can be from their own life or the life of a family member; most important, it should be a good story, one they have not minded hearing again and again over the years.

Important questions for critique: Is it always obvious who is performing the action and who is speaking? Does the story make sense? Is the tone of the story clear and consistent?

Chapter 29   Writing an Essay Using Process

When covering process writing this time, build on the foundation laid in Step Four and require students to continue to develop a more complex understanding of the pattern. You may wish to give students outlines detailing the type of structure and style you expect them to achieve. Here are a few examples that can be assigned individually or in groups:

1. Have students write a simple recipe directed to six-year-olds, the kind that might be found in a children's magazine. Students should write for the audience and anticipate any difficulties someone of that age group might encounter.

2. Ask students to write directions for making a grilled cheese sandwich for a military manual.

3. Ask students to supply instructions for a complicated, technical task in clear, straightforward language ("Changing Fuses for Dummies").

You might increase the level of difficulty even further by requiring students to write a narrative introduction and a call to action conclusion.

Chapter 30   Writing an Essay Using Comparison/Contrast

Strive to help students achieve higher levels of writing when working on comparison or contrast. You might want to have them write a sentence outline of the same two-part topic first using the block method then using point-by-point. Ask students to analyze both structures and decide which is a better approach for the given topics.

One of the most challenging tasks you can present to students is to have them write a comparison or contrast of two written works (any genre works well). Begin by handing out two paragraphs that you deem suitable. Have students read the paragraphs, identify the topic sentence in each, and write three-sentence summaries. Have students get into groups and discuss their opinions and eventually come up with a basic outline for comparing or contrasting the works. You will be in high demand during the exercise, so make yourself available by circling the groups. Ask students to write a three-paragraph comparison or contrast for homework, or, if time permits, in the remaining class period.

Chapter 31   Writing an Essay Using Persuasion

Most classes enjoy debating issues. Take advantage of this fact if you have a lively class when you begin the unit on persuasion. However, verbal debate tends to be much easier than written argument. Whenever you have sufficiently debated an issue in class, have students spend 10 to 15 minutes writing about the points that were discussed during the debate. You may even wish to have students freewrite on a given issue before the debate begins.

Magazine advertisements come in very handy when you need to give quick concrete examples of persuasive tactics. Find a variety of ads and let students pick those that appeal to them. Divide the board into two sections: text and visual. Have students identify every persuasive technique they see and read in the ad. Then require students to write a short analysis of the effectiveness of the persuasion in the ad they have chosen.

Chapter 32   Writing Under Pressure

All students need practice writing within time limits to force them to organize material and make choices quickly. The focus of the chapter is on the in-class essay, but students will find these skills valuable in all areas of their college careers. After working through the unit, give students several short, timed writing assignments. When they seem comfortable with the time restrictions, allow 35 minutes for the following exercise.

Have the students brainstorm on one of the following topic ideas:

1. Travel is broadening.

2. Gardening is hard work but pays in the end.

3. My grandparents' lives were quite difficult.

4. It is essential to be computer literate today.

5. Embarrassing moments can build character.

Divide the board into three sections and put the topic idea at the top of each section. In section one use the heading "Illustration," in section two use the heading "Process," and in section three use the heading, "Definition." Then lead the students through the manner in which the topic idea would be expressed differently in each of these paragraph modes. Have a good idea ahead of time what the finished product will look like. You may wish to have a finished copy of the three paragraphs ready to hand out at this stage so that you can go through each and show how each was based on the basic structure elucidated already on the board. Follow through by giving the students another list of topic ideas and have them write three more paragraphs using the same rhetorical modes.

This exercise works well as a longer group assignment and even better as a home journal assignment to be collected and revised. Play with different combinations of rhetorical modes: Cause and Effect/Narration/Classification and Division; or Description/Comparison and Contrast/Persuasion. It is a good idea to choose widely differing modes the first time this exercise is used and, if you choose to use it later in the semester, increase the level of difficulty by choosing the modes most easily confused: Description/Definition/Illustration, for example. When grading this assignment, note whether the student has:

1. employed transitional words and phrases appropriate to each mode,

2. changed the topic sentence in each case to suit the requirements of the given paragraph, and

3. maintained paragraph unity and fluid writing throughout.

Collaboration in the Developmental Writing Classroom

By DICK HARRINGTON
Piedmont Virginia Community College

Two related breakthroughs

During my twenty-nine years of teaching writing, two related discoveries have transformed my pedagogy: writing-as-a-process and collaboration—collaboration among peers and my own collaboration with my students. As *The Writer's Workplace* illustrates, in composition classes instructors now coach students through successive stages of revisions, helping them develop habits that improve all dimensions of their writing, from ideas to punctuation. The classroom has become a workshop. Students learn primarily by reading and discussing texts in progress, collaborating with the teacher and with one another.

Stages of writing

As in learning a sport or a musical instrument, it's useful to focus attention on certain elements at a given time and to attend to others later. With plenty of allowance for individual differences, I encourage students to view and practice writing in four broad, recursive stages: EXPLORING, DRAFTING, EDITING, and PROOFING. EXPLORING involves whatever precedes drafting: reading, note taking, cogitating, freewriting, clustering, or whatever works. DRAFTING establishes intention, voice, development, arrangement—the big picture. EDITING refines word choice, imagery, rhythm and flow of sentences, other points of style. PROOFING verifies convention (or intentional deviation) in grammar, usage, mechanics, documentation, and format. These stages are the foundation for meaningful collaboration with me as the teacher and with peers.

Stages and collaboration

Whether in developmental or college composition, learning and applying a regimen for each stage of the writing process engages students constructively with works in progress and enables students to develop awareness of audience—of how tone and other choices affect readers. They learn to talk about writing and therefore to think about it, with different emphases at each stage. They discover their own strengths and weaknesses, and they learn by example, seeing how others approach writing. They build genre awareness from the ground up. This kind of learning fosters responsibility and independence, particularly independence from the teacher, and allows students to take possession of their writing, spend more time on it, and generally experience greater success and satisfaction as writers. For all of this to develop, students must usually make quite an adjustment in their concept of roles in the classroom, both theirs and the teacher's. At the beginning of a semester students may expect the instructor to do most of the work during a class period, filling them up with what they need to know. For students to adapt and to contribute more in class it's essential for the instructor to adapt by encouraging students to participate more frequently.

Instructor moves to the side

To teach writing as a process and to employ peer work groups requires a profound shift in pedagogy and therefore in roles. In the traditional college classroom the instructor is the central figure, the most animated participant, and the hardest worker, lecturing, questioning, assigning, responding, and grading. Many students remain passive even when apparently listening and taking notes. In the collaborative classroom all students participate actively and indeed do most of the work. Each group becomes its own microcosm of the writing world. For this to happen, the instructor must move to the side and commit to student independence, to giving up control, to living with what may seem like chaos. At first, students feel incapable of helping one another or even of following the regimen for each stage, especially the DRAFTING stage. Although I do sit in on groups to coach them as they learn the regimens, as much as possible I let them be, trusting in the value of their ongoing engagement with texts in progress—mostly without me.[1] I prepare students thoroughly for the regimen of each stage, allowing plenty of time for each session, orchestrating but not controlling their discovery of how the group process works. While students work in groups, I mainly sit by myself, working on course-related matters and observing from a distance, awaiting signals for consultation. It's taken me a long time to adjust to this role of relative unimportance. Recently in a class just a few weeks old, as I walked among the groups to see if there were any questions or problems, they were so engaged that not one student looked up even to smile. Although my ultimate goal is for students not to need me, the reality of being ignored—however appropriately—takes some getting used to.

My developmental courses

My developmental courses begin with several introductory classes devoted to orientation, to the course, to group work, to getting acquainted, and to practical lessons in writing-as-a-process. On the first day, students take seats at small tables and find themselves already in groups of four or five facing one another rather than facing the front. Unless I see a problem with groups so selected, I let them remain as they are. Early in the course they engage in brief, purposeful group activities to get to know one another and to begin working together

---

[1] Successful collaboration requires careful planning.

cohesively. They exchange phone numbers and consider times to meet outside of class if necessary. We discuss writing as both a solitary and social activity, and I stress the necessity of hard work alone, such as reading, note taking, thinking, and producing good working drafts. I refer students to the bold, extra-large type in the course description and schedule, signaling the most important deadline of all: the class when the working draft of Paper 1 is to appear, without fail, no matter what, for presentation to the group. The course depends on such preparedness, good working drafts typed on a word processor with copies for the group.

After several days in the classroom, we meet in a reserved section of the computer lab for an introductory session on word processing and then several sessions of drafting and redrafting. The first paper assigned is a short essay on a social and/or personal issue developed from students' own thought and experience. While working at the keyboard, students can call me over for consultation about DRAFTING issues such as a main purpose, voice, development, and arrangement. I encourage students to overlook surface features and concentrate on rereading and thinking through their drafts. When ready, students print out a draft and sign up for a mini-conference in the lab. I skim the draft and coach them in rethinking and revising. By the scheduled deadline they produce a working draft for presentation to their peer group. Already they should be developing awareness that a draft for presentation to the group is not merely a freewrite, but the result of several hours of writing, coaching, rethinking, and rewriting.

Responding at the drafting stage

Responding at the DRAFTING stage requires the ability—and will—to comprehend whole drafts and help the writer see the big picture. Many developmental students must struggle very hard to read globally and respond constructively. To do so, they need time and in many cases privacy. I used to have students respond orally after listening to the draft read aloud and then reading it silently. The more I've observed and inquired about students' areas of difficulties with this procedure the more clearly I've understood their problems in comprehending a draft read aloud. I now have students take home the drafts and respond in writing, following the same prompt they will later use when responding at the moment. This same prompt helps writers respond to their own drafts, too, and prepares them to understand and consider the responses of others. An example of this prompt follows. At the next class meeting, the writers collect the responses to their drafts, read them thoughtfully, without conversation, and make notes toward revision. After perhaps half an hour, each writer gets five minutes to sum up and discuss his/her plans for revision. Early in the course, I request copies of responses, so that I can skim them and offer coaching where necessary. Because students are curious about the responses to their drafts, they tend to keep busy, although temptation lurks to converse all along. I want them to read silently and think on their own, so I foster relative quiet for that first half hour. When a group strays from appropriate behavior, I signal them from where I'm sitting or sit down with them and, preferably with humor, entice them back to the fold. Once, early in the term, after an immature, disruptive group continued to defy my enticements, I wrote to them on a big piece of paper and laid it face up on their table: "Act like adults or get out now." Once they realized I take this stuff seriously and expected them to, they transformed themselves into students and had a successful semester.

The prompt for the DRAFTING stage (originally adapted from Peter Elbow's "Giving Movies of Your Mind" and from his distinction between criterion-based and reader-based responding) is designed to promote spontaneous, natural conversation by which the writer gains insight about strengths and weaknesses, and feels enthusiasm for rewriting:

Prompt for the Drafting Stage

(1) Tell your experience of the draft—what it says and how it affects you. Intention? Audience? Tone? Arrangement? Development?

(2) Tell what strikes you as effective—ideas, phrases, images, etc.

(3) Tell what you'd like to know more about.

> Note: See the big picture. Neglect style, grammar, usage, mechanics, format, and other points treated later.

The first step in the regimen, by far the most lengthy and demanding, may incorporate the other two steps. The responder iterates the main intention of the piece and how it comes across as the piece develops. The response is a summary of both the draft as such and of the responder's thoughts and feelings in experiencing it. Addressing the writer directly, the responder creates connection with the writer and with what the writer is saying, even in areas where the draft breaks down. Telling what is actually there in the draft, what seems struggling to be there, and what the responder experiences helps the writer envision a likely focus and often the language with which to express it. Telling what seems especially effective helps the writer know what to build upon. Telling what the responder would like to know more about helps the writer sense what readers need to know or are interested in knowing. Throughout the process, responding as a reader reading seems much more helpful than giving advice.

Much of what the writer gains from a response comes not from advice, but from the language and feeling of the responder. Generative energy develops between responder and writer, and the writer imagines possibilities for rewriting. One word or phrase used by the responder may create an opening to insight. For this to happen, the writer must think intently, seeking ideas about rewriting. It's especially important to highlight whatever makes the writer feel defensive. Usually feelings of defensiveness are a sign of the writer's wanting to reject a truth being revealed. Later, that information may become essential in rewriting. Especially group members who are prone to defensiveness must train themselves to accept and consider whatever responders say. Following is an example of a working draft and reader-based response using the prompt for the DRAFTING stage. The student writer, S. J., is composing an essay on a social and/or personal issue, developed from her own thought and experience.

A sample draft by S. J.

Family Problems

Crack Cocaine been in our neighborhoods for more than ten years. The talk about crack have quieted down but the usage of the drug have only gotten worse, harming the life of those that uses it or be around it.

Crack stay inside the body for less than a week but it may stay a habit for many years. Crack have become a drug stronger and more addictive than any other drug on the streets. It take less time to become addicted to crack than any other drug. Crack have been the reason our society must deal with the crime wave that is sweeping our nation. We don't only have to worry about the addicted one. We also must worry about the ones that are dealing.

Crack is a hard drug to cure yourself from. Most addict usually relapse over and over again. Most crack addict return to smoking because they feel that there is nowhere for them to turn to. Often family members let them think that no one know what they are doing, so they continue using drugs.

Crack have taken over my family in more ways than one. The only thing that crack has done for my family is torn it apart. I have had to bail family members out of all kinds of trouble. If they were to use their minds as much as they use the drug, they would not be getting in so many mishaps.

In my family there has been a bad drug problem. My family don't have to worry only about the drug user, we also have to worry about the drug dealers in the family. When you have drug users and dealer's in one family things can get very hard to deal with. Most of the time we must worry about whether some of our family members will make it home alive or unharmed.

When a family member is on drugs it is sometimes hard to believe it. It may be because your don't want to believe what is going on. You may notice that a family member is acting funny or starting to steal things from around the house. At first you may not want to say or do anything about it, but we all know that something must be done about the drug problem.

I have gotten to the point that I will not trust my children with my uncle. I'm afraid that he might neglect them in some way. He is into drugs real bad. Most of the time I don't trust him in my house. I'm afraid that he might steal something from me.

When you have a dealer and user in the same family they both usually watch one another back, so that no one will find out what is going on. The dealer will give the drug to the user so that no one in the family will find out there are selling drugs. The addict will take the drug because most of the time it is coming free. Sometime this can end up as a big problem. The dealer must keep account for what he have giving away. If not the person that he is selling the drugs for will take the payment out on the dealer.

There was this time when my cousin was selling drugs and my uncle was the addict. My cousin would give my uncle the drugs he wanted so that he wouldn't go back and tell that he was selling drugs. My uncle started getting used to my cousin giving him drugs. One day my uncle couldn't find my cousin so he decided to go in the bed room and just take the drugs he wanted. My uncle didn't realize that my cousin would get in trouble for that.

My cousin knew who had taken the drug but there was nothing that he could say or do. The next day when my cousin got home he told us that he had been beaten up by some guys who didn't like him. I knew what had really happen to him.

My family try to act like they don't know what is going on but they do. A few years later my cousin was sent to prison. He was charged as a drug Kingpin and sentenced to thirty-six years. My uncle is still in and out using drugs all the time bringing his family down more and more each time he spend his pay check and get into trouble.

Solving this drug problem must start within the home. Families need to try to help one another with there problem and stop over looking it.

A sample reader-based response (written) to S. J.'s draft

J. D. Telling Her Experience of the Draft, What Strikes Her as Effective, and What She Wants to Know More About

I feel the main idea of your paper is how dangerous crack can become and how it affects the family. It was very interesting to see how crack can work from within a family out into the community. You point out and clearly show how crack can affect family member's trust and how it breaks down the family unit. For example, when you mention how your cousin gave your uncle crack, for free, in order not to be exposed to the family. I can empathize with you on why you would not trust certain family members and how this could harm your family. I feel you develop the paper nicely and show what crack is and bring in how it effects the family. I definitely see your point on how drug abuse has started at home and treating the problem needs to begin at home, as well.

I found your paper to be very interesting and felt very connected with you when you talked about how it has affected your life and family. I certainly can see you would like to see the problem stopped and agree that families need to help each other. I was able to follow your paper and clearly see where it was going. Personally, I feel you were very courageous to write about this topic and how you bring out your family. It seems that you really want to help make a change and wish you luck. I enjoyed reading your paper and it did touch me, as far as, making me aware of how crack can hurt a family.

My analysis of J. D.'s response to S. J.'s draft

As a novice responder, J. D. does a good job of identifying and recounting the main purpose and effect of the draft. I like how she connects with the writer, addressing S. J. directly, revealing how the draft touches her as a reader and teaches her about cocaine in families. I like how she focuses on the big picture, as instructed, and neglects any mention of editing or proofreading issues. I like how she recalls a specific example from the text to illustrate what seems effective. Apparently, she feels satisfied with the scope and coverage of the piece, because she doesn't mention anything she'd like to know more about.

In helping J. D. learn to respond even more constructively, I focus on two elements: (1) As she summarizes the piece and recounts her experience of it, I want her to reveal the arrangement of parts as well as the means of development, and help the writer see how the introduction and body might focus the reader's attention more directly on the main purpose. (2) I want her to use the language of the prompt more deliberately so both responder and writer know whether she is telling her experience of the piece, or telling what strikes her as effective, or telling what she wants to know more about. While it's fine to intermix the three elements rather than divide them artificially, I want the responder to consider each element deliberately and to respond specifically. Recounting her experience of the piece should include audience and tone, which J. D. doesn't mention. Telling what strikes her as effective should involve saying back, often word for word, the outstanding passages. Telling what she wants to know more about should involve deliberate consideration of the scope and coverage of the piece. In this instance, J. D. should acknowledge directly that the piece feels complete.

Need for teacher intervention

Her response reveals the need for teacher intervention at the DRAFTING stage—to coach each group in responding and to coach the writer in learning what to do with peer responses. J. D.'s response well identifies the main purpose and spirit of the piece (although I want her to see that the piece primarily recounts the effects of drug use on the family; while prevention of drug use may need to begin in the family, the primary intention of the piece is not to develop a solution). Given such responses and coaching, S. J. can learn to reread her draft, imagine reader expectations from the opening sentences, decide whether her introduction establishes the intended purpose, and revise more deliberately. Ideally, J. D.'s response helps cause the writer S. J. to think for herself, "Aha, the effect of cocaine on families is my main intention, isn't it? Now I see what I need to work on to focus and unify my piece."

Such responding is hard and takes lots of practice

To provide ideal responses, students need considerable coaching, practice, and concentration. It's difficult for some to articulate the primary intention of even a published article. Doing so for a working draft sometimes requires locating evidence of a primary intention that is only partially realized or ambivalent. I discuss this challenge—grasping main ideas—as part of the lifelong process of developing ourselves as readers and thinkers. In the struggle to read globally and respond constructively, they improve their reading comprehension, learning over time to see the big picture rather than smaller elements. Ultimately (as E. D. Hirsch once mentioned in a seminar) students can write only so well as they can read their own writing. And of course, as they freewrite their responses at home (or in the computer lab), they gain practice in expressing themselves on paper, and they develop abilities needed for responding extemporaneously later in the course and in college composition. At first, some students, especially the self-conscious or shy, may feel uncomfortable communicating what feels like criticism. As they develop this ability, they learn to reveal a draft's shortcomings honestly—but diplomatically and constructively—from their perspective as readers. The writer learns to consider what each group member says. Students learn that even the least accomplished or perceptive group member may provide useful information. They also come to understand that writing need not and cannot be just a leap in the dark. It's a process of rewriting.

Responding orally at the drafting stage

Later in the course, as students improve their ability to read globally, ideally they can begin to respond orally at the moment rather than taking drafts home and writing their responses. I say "ideally" because I've tended to postpone such expectation until college composition (even there, students need to practice by writing responses at home). A good intermediate step is for them to read the drafts at home and then to respond orally in the next class period after the writer reads once aloud. In an oral session at the DRAFTING stage, the writer reads the draft aloud once at a natural pace while other group members follow along and make notes on their copy. Then they take a few minutes to read silently and make more notes. The member to the left of the writer responds orally for two minutes, using as a guide the prompt for the DRAFTING stage. In turn, each group member responds likewise for two minutes, regardless of how much others' responses are repeated. A monitor keeps time and helps keep members on track. With practice, groups can cover four shorter papers in a class period (if I don't talk too much at the beginning). The writer listens, makes extensive notes, and keeps quiet, quelling the urge to justify a passage criticized or to talk about the subject. I emphasize writing down whatever feels uncomfortable, living with it for a while, and then deciding whether revision is appropriate.

At the start of class when the working draft is due for oral presentation and responses, students set a copy on my desk and give each group member a copy. While they work together, I skim each draft looking for focus, development, and arrangement. I usually bracket the main idea/intention and supporting points as I go and then at the end summarize the idea/intention. If the draft seems adequate as a draft, I return it to the writer without suggestions, trusting the group process to generate thoughtful revision. If the draft feels inadequate as a draft, lacks focus, is undeveloped, or seems disorganized, then I usually outline what's there and suggest what might need to happen during rewriting in order to fulfill the apparent intention. Because I intervene only when I see real problems, the groups tend to maintain independence from me. They don't negate group responses, expecting that I'll present "the real truth." This boundary is essential—as is my intervening when appropriate. By the end of the hour, I've usually read and returned all the drafts, and the groups have usually completed their responses and note taking. One or two students will usually seek help from me in resolving conflicting responses. Sometimes I help best by clarifying their options and saying, "The decision is up to you, the writer." Other times I reveal what seems an effective choice.

Redrafting and editing

Now it's the solitary job of each student to consider our sometimes conflicting responses, to rethink and rewrite as much as is needed for presenting at the next class a draft that is better focused, better developed, better arranged, and more consciously edited. Accomplished mainly with the ear and eye, EDITING refines the style or character of a piece. I want them to understand that good writing engages readers and pleases us aesthetically, like music. The notes work together to create one purposeful effect. While students have no doubt edited some along the way, they have attended mainly to the big picture. Now they consider each word, each phrase or image, each sentence, each cluster of sentences, each paragraph—all in relation to the focal intention. I model the EDITING process and provide practice in reading the text aloud and responding to the writer's stylistic choices. To help attune their eyes and ears, I suggest reading into a tape recorder and then listening while editing. Students who do so often report astonishment at what they discover.

In the class period devoted to EDITING, they provide a copy for each group member (but not for me). They divide the class period into four units of about twelve minutes, one for each writer. The writer reads one paragraph aloud and then awaits responses, which don't involve a set prompt or order. Responders are encouraged to bring up anything that nags at them: a vague generalization in the opening, a cliché, a seemingly highfalutin Latinate noun, inappropriate choppiness of rhythm. The group tries not to rewrite but to help the writer see where refinements of style might be appropriate. For one thing, the writer needs to learn by doing. For another, a group might spend the whole time bogged down in one sentence. The writer makes notes, especially about observations that feel uncomfortable. When that writer's time is up, the group moves on to the next member's paper, even if not completed with the former. During such EDITING sessions, students tend to work appropriately for the whole period because the task is well defined, practical, engaging, and challenging. Many seem fascinated, never having attended so deliberately to stylistic choices in relation to purpose and effect. They learn to notice and articulate how choices affect them. At the end of the period, they now face the solitary job of applying what they have learned to the refinement of their paper. After doing so, they proof it as best they can and make whatever changes seem necessary, in preparation for the class period devoted to proofing.

Proofing

The Scarry text offers practical lessons on common proofing problems, and I've found that as students produce successive revisions and work in groups, they tend to employ and build on their tacit knowledge of language, which is usually much greater than they or we realize. Many surface errors are the result of inattention rather than ignorance. As students attend to their own texts and the texts of others, they make more and more corrections of nonstandard forms and come to grasp and apply more and more conventions of college writing. They identify what they don't know, such as the distinction between *lie* and *lay,* and they explore how to learn such distinctions (*The Writer's Workplace,* handbook, dictionary, grammar check, spell check, conversation with group members or me). They also learn that different readers have different expectations or preconceptions about "correctness," that proofing choices depend partly on intention and audience, not on set rules. Some students have been taught "Never use *I*" or "Never use contractions," while others have been taught to use *I* when referring to themselves or to use *don't* to help establish a conversational interaction with the reader, even in fairly formal writing.

If there is enough time, the writer presents the whole paper to the whole group for PROOFING. My students prefer doing so because they get more eyes and ears involved. To save time, however, I often have them work in groups of two, each with a copy. One partner reads the piece aloud naturally but slowly. Both try to keep their eyes and minds focused on each successive element, listening and looking for "errors." Some sentences have to be reread and reexamined. Either partner is encouraged to bring up whatever might be a problem, the point being to engage in conversation about proofing issues that will help each writer learn what to look for and how to make corrections in the future. If the partners can't resolve an issue by discussing it or by consulting the handbook, a raised hand brings me to their table for a consultation. Sometimes I can resolve a question directly: "Yes, you do need a comma there to prevent misreading." Other times I'm moved to say, "It depends. Journalists leave out the comma before *and* in a series, while academic writers include it. I prefer its inclusion because it sets off the elements clearly. Your main concerns are to be consistent throughout your paper and to make choices that don't call attention to themselves. Since right now you're focusing on college writing, I recommend including the comma before *and* in a series." The best students, because they raise so many proofing issues, will sometimes take a whole class period for two papers, first the one partner's and then the other's.

The writer keeps a master copy and is the only one who writes on it, deciding whether or not to make a suggested change or correction, assuming full responsibility for the text. Students learn and remember more by thinking about and writing the suggested change. Also, they would in effect be cheating if someone else, including me, actually made corrections for them, instead of raising issues for discussion and learning. During PROOFING sessions students tend to stay focused because—as with the ending sessions—the work is well defined, practical, engaging, and challenging. When students do stray, I can usually bring them back by approaching them and saying in good humor something like "Here come the writing police." I must say that in both developmental and college composition, such PROOFING sessions have transformed my job of reading "finished" papers. After the second or third paper of the term in developmental, it's not unusual for me to have to mark as few as five or six items in a paper, a comma here, a capital letter there. It's a pleasure to read and respond as a reader rather than as a marker. Of course, some students may require even more intensive intervention than the PROOFING sessions and the systematic lessons in *The Writer's Workplace* can provide.

The "finished" paper

Now students make all necessary refinements in form and then in the next class period submit the paper for my evaluation. Unlike some of my colleagues in the profession who are rightly determined to de-emphasize grades, I do put a "grade" on each "finished" paper. It lets students know where they stand in an imperfect academic world where grades are the norm. It also serves as an incentive to rewrite for a higher grade. At my college, developmental courses are graded *Satisfactory* or *Unsatisfactory* (essentially *Pass* or *Fail*). Sometimes I'll write, among other comments, "An excellent paper. *S* if you correct the one comma splice and prove to me you understand the principle." Often the student will say to the group, "I still don't understand this comma splice thing. Can you help me?" And of course what happens is the whole group explores the issue.

Much for the teacher to learn

I began by asserting that writing-as-a-process and peer work groups constitute the two most important breakthroughs in my twenty-nine years of teaching. Some crusty, seasoned colleagues dismiss such notions out of hand: "Just more educational fads," they mutter, "nothing more than the swing of the pendulum." I would argue, conversely, that we're developing these concepts and practices from substantial, documented observations of how writers actually work. Unlike most beginners, seasoned writers expect to rewrite. Writers develop habits of revision that enable discovery, revelation, and refinement. Writers also employ trusted readers whose responses help to validate or redirect the writing. We're also becoming aware that learning to write is something like learning a sport. Students need coaching and training, but most of all, they need to get out there daily and play the game. If you don't like the sports analogy, then consider sculpting. The sculpting class is a workshop in which the teacher demonstrates principles, students work on their own pieces, and all engage in ongoing critiques of works in progress. The more I learn about coaching students as writers writing and readers responding, the more I value this pedagogy and the more I realize I'm just beginning to understand its possibilities. It puts students at the very center of what we have always wanted them to master.

Using the World Wide Web to Create a Learner-Centered Classroom

By MARLA DINCHAK

Glendale Community College—Glendale, Arizona

**presented at NISOD 1999 International Conference
on Teaching & Leadership Excellence**

While educators are familiar with the World Wide Web as a presentation medium, many are unaware of its value as a learning tool in the classroom. This presentation will explain the practical application of the World Wide Web as a primary tool to create a learner-centered classroom.

Introduction

The mission of the community college is focused on meeting the educational needs of the people living within its geographical boundaries. This community includes recent high school students, reentry students preparing for new careers or job changes, and students seeking technical skills, as well as remedial students and special-interest students. The mission of Maricopa Community Colleges is to "strive to exceed the changing expectation of our many communities for effective, innovative, student-centered, flexible and lifelong educational opportunities." As the needs of the community change, the effective community college must anticipate these needs, developing programs and courses to prepare students for a rapidly changing world. Traditional teaching methods need to be examined and new, innovative approaches considered for teaching and learning.

In his book, *A Learning College for the 21st Century* (Phoenix: American Council on Education/Oryx Press Series on Higher Education, 1997), Terry O'Banion calls for a new model of education for the community college called the "learning college." This model places learning, and the learner, first in the order of priorities. The learning college is based on six key principles:

- The learning college creates substantive change in individual learners.
- The learning college engages learners as full partners in the learning process, with learners assuming primary responsibility for their own choices.
- The learning college creates and offers as many options for learning as possible.
- The learning college assists learners to form and participate in collaborative learning activities.
- The learning college defines the roles of learning facilitators by the needs of the learners.
- The learning college and its learning facilitators succeed only when improved and expanded learning can be documented for its learners.

These assumptions consider the learner first, before other issues. MCCCD has made a commitment to a learner-centered paradigm ("Toward Becoming a Learner-Centered College System," Paul A. Elsner, January 1996). Emphasis throughout the Maricopa district is on the learner. Putting theory into practice,

I have taken the concept of a learner-centered paradigm into my freshman composition classroom. My goal is to create a learner-centered classroom. The World Wide Web is a most useful tool to accomplish this goal.

The World Wide Web as a learning tool

The WWW seems to be everywhere—on TV, in newspapers and magazines, and on our desktops. This technology tool has rapidly exploded upon the mainstream of our lives in just a few years. Students entering the college classroom are familiar with the Web from television advertisements, the media, and their own computing experiences. All have heard of the Web, and most students have clicked from Web site to Web site at home or their workplace. The visual aspects of the Web are enticing, the point-and-click environment is easy to use, and the communication capabilities are enormous, as seen by the rapid growth of business and commercial Web sites.

The obvious value of the Web in education is as a delivery method for course materials. Course syllabi, assignments, calendars and due dates are posted on many teacher Web sites, easily accessible from multiple locations. Placing course materials on a Web site provides flexibility and convenience for both students and teachers. However, this is simply a technological way to disperse information traditionally presented in a print format. In many cases, very few changes even occur from the print to the digital presentation. In reality, the technology is an "add-on" to the traditional course of instruction rather than a substantive change in instruction.

In the past several years I've developed a half-dozen complex Web sites and, in the process, learned a great deal about how to learn. At that time, there were no college classes or seminars available to teach me Web page development, so I taught myself from materials on the Web and in collaboration with colleagues. Upon reflection, I realize that the nature of the Web itself changed the way I thought and learned about writing. My writing became tighter, more focused, concise. The effect of the communication became more important than the individual paragraphs and pages. My audience was real and responsive, which motivated me to try new and innovative ways to communicate. I learned to ask for assistance when I couldn't figure out a particularly thorny problem. Collaboration with colleagues also learning to use this new technology was invaluable. I became a more confident, independent learner, a skill I want to share with my students.

My goal of creating a learner-centered classroom required a new approach. Since I was already teaching in a networked classroom, technology tools were available. However, the computers in the English networked classrooms were used, for the most part, for word-processing, some e-mail interaction, and cursory Web searches for source material. The networked classroom computers provide students with Internet access through Netscape, disk space on the Web for Web pages, e-mail, and an assortment of software for word processing and other activities. Obviously, we had been underutilizing this tool.

My goal of creating a learner-centered classroom is primarily accomplished by using student-created Web sites as an interactive learning tool. My students use the Web as a learning tool, creating their own Web sites to publish their writing, connecting with their classmates and others, and practicing learning skills. The technology invites active participation and collaboration, and provides immediate feedback to stimulate and encourage learners. The visible results displayed on a student-created Web site provide documented feedback to students of their own learning progress. The Web in my learner-centered classroom is much more than a way to distribute a course syllabus; it is the primary tool to teach students how to learn from each other and independently.

Six key elements of the learning classroom

The learning classroom creates substantive change in individual learners

A goal in my freshman writing course is for students to learn to communicate written ideas clearly, logically, and effectively. Students write five assignments for print and then rewrite those assignments and publish them on their own Web site, called a Web Portfolio. In publishing these written assignments to Web pages, the students learn the differences between effective communication in both the written and the digital medium. For example, they soon realize that a printed, extended essay does not communicate as effectively when placed on the Web. The nature of the electronic medium, and the expectations of the audience, require a different type of written communication and encourages visual presentation of ideas.

Moreover, students learn to think about writing in a different way—as a communication tool that can be manipulated to best suit different audiences and presentations. They begin to understand the power of the written word, and that this is a tool they can use to communicate their own ideas to a real audience. Computer-assisted writing encourages revision and changes, as it is very easy to try out different presentations and approaches. Thus, students readily experiment with words, sentences and paragraphs to create new texts and place them on their Web sites for their classmates and the world to view. The feedback they get from each other and from others outside the classroom reinforces the concept of writing as a communication tool they can use in the real world.

The learning classroom engages learners as full partners in the learning process, with learners assuming primary responsibility for their own choices

The democratizing of the classroom is one step toward creating a learner-centered environment. The integration of technology in the classroom creates changes in learners and teachers. Teachers become learners, and students learn to teach. The teacher's willingness to become a learner is essential. Technological changes in our society have been swift, and many teachers find themselves unprepared to use the new technology, let alone integrate it into their courses. This may be unsettling, unless the teacher can adopt the role of learner. The teacher is no longer the primary source of information, but a valuable resource and facilitator in the classroom. This major shift in roles from the traditional student-teacher relationship creates a substantive change in student also. The student, not the teacher, becomes the focus of the classroom experiences; learning, not teaching, becomes the primary goal in the classroom. This new partnership of learners teaches students how to learn from many resources: their peers, as well as their teacher, their textbooks, and technological resources.

While technology creates a level playing field for learners and teachers alike, the student-created Web sites provide many opportunities for students to take responsibility and make choices. Technology is an engaging phenomenon, inviting people to push buttons, click and participate in all sorts of interactive activities. Unlike the traditional classroom lecture, where students passively listen, the computer classroom requires students to actively participate and interact with the software on the monitor. The Web is a rich source of information for writing, but this is a passive activity not much different from reading a textbook. On the other hand, creating a Web site is a highly engaging activity, requiring students to manipulate software to produce text and images on a monitor that can be constantly changed and revised to produce a different effect. The student must make dozens of choices that result in the page on his or her screen. The exercise requires judgment and critical thought and provides instant feedback.

The learning classroom creates and offers as many options for learning as possible

Using the Web offers many options on different levels for students and teachers alike. Students are not place-bound and have access to course materials in the networked classroom, in the computer labs on campus, and at home if they have a computer. While over 60 percent of our students have computers at home, computers are available for students to use outside class. Our campus has two computer labs with over 400 computers available to students 7 days a week, from 7 A.M. to midnight. I've placed course assignments, calendars, tutorials and help guides for software, and much more on the course Web site for students to access 24 hours a day. Students and teachers are linked via e-mail giving students access to help and support both in and out of the classroom.

The Web allows students to experiment with different learning styles from the traditional lecture-delivered information. The Web is highly interactive. Students seem to enjoy manipulating things, clicking to different Web sites searching for information and experimenting with search engines and new ways to find information. Additionally, the knowledge base available on the Web is wide and varied, giving students access to resources and sites related to specific topics. Because the technology is relatively new, and few students have created Web pages previously, they are encouraged to teach and learn from each other as well as from course information and other Web sites. Students actually learn how to learn, a skill they can transfer to all other areas of their lives.

The learning classroom assists learners to form and participate in collaborative learning activities

Learning with the Web and student-created Web sites is a new experience for the majority of students. The course materials and tutorials are available on the Web, but students quickly realize that their best source of help and support is the person sitting next to them! This in itself encourages collaboration as the students learn their way around the Web and create their own Web pages.

The nature of the Web is linked and cooperative. The hyperlinks that are the basics of its dynamic nature connect ideas and the people who create them. My students create Web sites that they link to their classmates' Web sites as well as to other sites in the world. They must work together to accomplish this, and they begin to realize that the world works collaboratively, too. Discussions in the classroom are often continued outside the classroom in electronic discussion groups as they learn that collaboration is not cheating, but a positive and effective way to learn.

The learning classroom defines the roles of learning facilitators by the needs of the learners

My role as teacher has evolved and merged into one of learner, facilitator, coach, and mentor. I've learned to create and revise Web pages by watching students interact with the course materials. I have created an environment which challenges students to learn new skills. Using these course materials, students discern relevance of and through the activities, develop writing skills, develop logical and critical thinking skills, and learn computer skills.

Using the Web as a primary learning tool has changed my in-class time, too. I use less class time for information delivery as the materials, readings, and resources are on each student's computer. I use the Web projected by a data show onto a screen in the classroom for presentations that are clear and easily accessed after class for review. Much of my classroom time is spent guiding students in interacting with materials I've selected for them on the Web. We work together to solve problems in writing, Web page creation, and using the Web. My role is less authoritarian, more supportive, and closer aligned with my personal teaching style.

Because the Web technology is new to many students, they have many questions and problems as they publish their writing. I have redefined my work time and now check e-mail frequently during the weekend and other times to answer student questions. While this might be a problem for some, I enjoy the flexibility of answering e-mail from home and don't confine my contact with students to office hours only. The college administration has been supportive of flexible hours and allows me to fulfill some office hour requirements by telecommuting from home.

The learning classroom and its learning facilitators succeed only when improved and expanded learning can be documented for its learners

Student Web portfolios provide documentation of improved and expanded learning that is obvious to students. My students publish all of their writing through the semester in their Web portfolios. Even though they are encouraged to constantly revise and modify their writing, all students at the end of the semester look back at what they have written and complete a self-assessment of their work. Invariably, they conclude that they have grown and learned as writers when they compare their first assignments with their final writings.

Another method of assessment is the questionnaire that all of our campus computer-assisted writing students fill out about midway through the semester. Students answer questions about their use of computers in the writing classroom and provide information as to how they feel it has helped them in their course work. The results of these questionnaires over the years have shown that more and more of our students have computers, feel that the computer makes writing easier for them, and prefer to take future writing classes with a computer. Many comments from my own students indicate that they enjoy the Web-based delivery of materials and like creating Web sites.

My own personal experiences with creating Web sites have resulted in improved and expanded learning which I have documented by saving older versions of Web sites I've created. A comparison of the original English department Web site I created with the current Web site shows an increased perception of organizational strategy, more concise writing, and a heightened awareness of audience. All of these are writing skills I now feel I can better teach to my students after learning them through creating a Web site. I now teach my students using the same tool that I found so effective for my own learning, the World Wide Web.

A few related Web sites

Marla's Place
   http://glory.gc.maricopa.edu/~mdinchak/welcome.htm

Welcome to ENG101 (course homepage)
   http://glory.gc.maricopa.edu/~mdinchak/eng101/index.htm

Glendale Community College, Glendale, AZ
   http://www.gc.maricopa.edu/

Dr. Paul Elsner, Chancellor, MCCCD
   http://www.dist.maricopa.edu/users/elsner/

The Learning College: Both Learner and Learning Centered by Terry O'Banion
   http://www.league.org/lelabs0399.html

A Learning College for the 21st Century by Terry O'Banion
   http://www.ntlf.com/html/lib/lc21_bio.htm

Incorporating Computer Literacy Into the Composition Classroom

By JOANNE REIN

According to James Berlin, "All truths arise out of dialectic, out of the interaction of individuals within discourse communities" (16-7). Along the same lines, he states, "These truths, after all, concern basic ethical and political decisions that affect the safety of all: they concern the distribution of power in legislatures, the courts, and social groups. In arriving at decisions about these matters, science and logic can be helpful, but ultimately choices are made on the basis of public discourse—individuals working together within a community of discourse trying to decide what will be in the best interests of the group and the individual" (15). Berlin supplements his theory with a discussion of the special relationship that exists between the human mind and nature. He recognizes a direct link that connects the human mind to the environment in which we live. In effect, he acknowledges that it is more than coincidental that we perceive reality according to how our minds are structured. Indeed, we can understand reality only in a manner consistent with how our minds are structured simply because we do not acknowledge what we cannot comprehend. Cross-linking composition theory with psychological studies done by Jerome Bruner and Jean Piaget, Berlin suggests that there can be a cognitive approach to rhetoric. Furthermore, he implies, "The epistemology of these rhetorics assumes a correspondence between the structure of the mind and the structure of nature" (16). This is the point at which Berlin provides a springboard for rhetoric and composition studies in the computer environment because these structures of mind and nature are rapidly changing in our technological era.

The information superhighway, inclusive of the Internet, the World Wide Web, e-mail, and all other current modes of communication have created for us a new nature, that of virtual reality. It is this new mode of communication for which we must prepare our students in a first-year composition classroom. No longer is paper-based essay instruction sufficient to render a student competent in either academia or the workplace. In fact, students must now be proficient in techniques of composing such as hypertext and the recursive writing process in order to perform various writing and research tasks as a prerequisite to success in both the classroom and on the job. It is our responsibility as writing instructors, therefore, to ensure that first-year students acquire these once peripheral skills that now are essential to survival in these technological times.

To provide our students with the up-to-date skills that they need to survive in our competitive and technological global community, it is essential that we investigate the underlying issues that govern how, why and to whom composition is taught in our classrooms today, as the first step toward providing a quality composition curriculum. In placing the composition classroom under scrutiny via cultural analysis, we can arrive at assumptions that allow us to take action toward progressive teaching strategies that recognize and accommodate the cultural factors of ethnicity, gender, and socioeconomic position of the student because these factors play a gargantuan role in a student's ability to compete, never mind to excel, in academia and ultimately the global community. Although a discussion of ethnicity and gender is beyond the scope of this essay, an awareness of socioeconomic position is integral to any discussion that seeks to explore computer literacy in the composition classroom. Without recognition of the problems of access to computers, teaching strategies in the composition classroom will be unproductive because they will only circumvent the real issue, instead of facing it directly, with a goal to eradicate the discrepancies that cause some students to arrive on campus more fluent in computer literacy than others. In approaching a study of composition theory in this manner we can anticipate and render harmless factors which serve to hinder student achievement in and out of the classroom. Also, addressing the very real phenomenon of socioeconomic position is a valid intervention method to ensure that all students have access to the global community that has evolved suddenly and in which they must compete, either willingly or by default.

Such a sociological and anthropological approach reveals that a trend common in most real time environments, or reality, exists also in cyberspace. In effect, obvious discrepancies exist and serve to divide our global community once again into socioeconomic elites and those subcommunities of individuals left out of the dominant culture. Basically, the cybercommunity is a society of haves and have-nots, although it could be an avenue toward equality if all members of the global community had equal access to it. The issue here is that if truth "arises out of dialectic, out of interaction of individuals within discourse communities" (16-7), as Berlin purports, but not all individuals have access to the dialogue that occurs in the global community of cyberspace because they cannot afford to purchase the medium necessary to participate, namely a computer, then is truth ever attained? Is equality ever attained? To rephrase these two questions another way, whose voice is not heard in our global community?

Following that argument, the best interests of the group as a whole or the individual members of the group are not served if only those members of the group that have access to the medium for dialogue are able to participate in the formulation of truth. The implications of denied access to the cyber community are relevant to the composition classroom in that computer literacy has replaced literacy as the means to an individual's ability to compete in both the classroom and the workplace. Without access to the equipment, and without the training to use the equipment, if access is eventually acquired, a student will not be able to perform the essential tasks necessary to complete, or even begin, the requirements for a college degree. That access and training must occur in the first-year composition classroom if it had not occurred prior to arrival on campus.

Current trends in the global community cause consumers to believe they must possess the latest technologies available. To keep pace with the times, computer vendors aggressively sell their latest products to everyone they can convince that the latest model is the only way to stay one step ahead of the competition in the business world. Schools also focus on this key element. After all, schools must keep pace with the outside world in order to serve their students' best interests, which are to provide them with the knowledge and the skills that will place them in the workforce. However, are the students' best interests served merely by purchasing the latest innovation if neither the students nor the instructors know how to use that latest innovation for all it is worth? Has the institution bought into a consumer economy without questioning its purpose for doing so or assessing its ability to engage its students in the new reality that is created by all of these advances in technology? Has the institution considered its students' computer fluency before sitting them down in front of the keyboard? It is grand to be able to state in the recruitment literature that the institution has a homepage and an e-mail address for every student that wants one, but not every student sees the urgency of this bit of propaganda because not every student is aware of the urgency of becoming a vocal member of the global community. It is also a wonderful reflection on the school to be able to announce that there is an abundance of computer laboratories on campus for student use, and all these laboratories have Pentium computers with CD-ROMs and speakers. So what of it, especially if the students cannot find their way through the Windows 95 screen to access Corel WordPerfect? Not one of those innovations is going to enable the students to get their essays written and handed in on time if they cannot find the right keys on the keyboard. This is a serious and very real issue for many first-year students in today's information age when the ability to access information electronically is vital to performance in the classroom and on the job.

Nonetheless, the first-year student is required to use the computer in not only his or her composition classroom, but in most of his or her other courses as well. The composition classroom, then, becomes a cross-training arena for writing and computer keyboarding. Reality dictates that without instruction in basic computer keyboarding, the student cannot succeed in the composition classroom. In addition, computer keyboarding by itself will not benefit the student in the composition classroom because computer keyboarding does not teach the writing process. However, the strategic combination of computer keyboarding and the writing process creates the sum total of a redefinition of computer literacy to the extent that computer literacy moves beyond the keyboard into document development through a recursive writing process that incorporates efficient use of the features of computer software to enhance the students' productivity at the keyboard.

Once productivity is enhanced, time spent on the works in progress is realigned to be used more effectively. For example, students who previously may have been reluctant to proofread now develop the habit of proofreading more readily because changes to documents can be made with a minimal amount of effort, as opposed to the major chore it would have been years ago when the manual typewriter was considered a luxury.

Also, the spell-check feature of word processing software encourages the students to take risks in relation to attempting to use vocabulary that they may not ordinarily use without the aid of the spell-check feature because they know that if they misspell a word, the computer has a high likelihood of flagging the error and providing them with the option to correct it. In paper-based essay writing, students will generally limit themselves to only those words they feel confident in spelling without the benefit of a dictionary because looking up words in a dictionary can be a tedious process.

In addition, stopping to look up a word in the middle of a thought can cause the thought to vanish, so another advantage of the spell-check feature in word processing software is that the writer can continue with the thought and correct the spelling errors later. This releases the writer from product-specific writing, meaning that the writer recognizes that the essay in production is not a finished product, but, indeed, a work in progress. The result is that the writer understands from the onset that the essay is to be revised. Hence, the process of writing is evident, and perceived as necessary, by the student.

Another aspect of computer-based writing is that the essay, being composed on the computer screen, is created in a neat, orderly font, or type, with margins automatically preset at the appropriate width and the page length always on display, as opposed to a possibly illegible handwritten first draft scribbled on scrap paper and marked through with revisions as found in paper-based writing. The student is able to visualize the final draft more readily in computer-based writing, thereby becoming encouraged through positive reinforcement, an educational technique that seems to be the most conducive to learning in any discipline.

Although computer-based writing is the most productive means to a finished product, there are problems for students who have not had the socioeconomic advantage of prior computer experience. In effect, these students are in jeopardy of losing ground in the global community due to their computer illiteracy.

As a result, the teaching strategies in my composition classroom are geared toward laboratory experiences with ample hands-on time at the computer. Since the primary purpose in my composition course is to help students reduce writing anxiety, it appears that writing in an electronic environment would only hinder this objective and amplify any writing anxiety already in existence. This is obviously counterproductive unless the electronic writing anxiety is overcome alongside simple writing anxiety. To ensure that my students do overcome any electronic writing anxiety they may experience, I try to anticipate those trouble spots in their electronic writing process that will block success. In effect, I incorporate some details of how computers operate in order to provide my students with an understanding of the various computer malfunctions and inappropriate computer techniques that could cause them to be unsuccessful in essay production.

For instance, the first assignment my students must do is to learn how to use WordPerfect. Not only must they achieve a satisfactory degree of competency using the software, they must also reach a level of competency in using the equipment, including troubleshooting computer problems such as printer jams and disk damage. This task seems simple enough, until certain factors are taken into consideration. The first obstacle to success occurs when a student has no disk on which to save his or her work. That is, indeed, the student's responsibility, but many students do not understand the importance of the disk until it is too late. The second mishap that occurs is when the student does not know how to format a disk. This can pose a problem if there is no computer technician around to assist. However, the ultimate goal in computer literacy is to become self-sufficient, not computer technician dependent.

Third, if the student is able to get through the first two hurdles, but saves his or her document on the hard drive instead of on his or her disk, that student's anxiety level can be expected to rise and a distaste for computer technology can overshadow any need to produce quality essays. Only through hands-on experience at the computer keyboard will students develop a routine that enables them to perform the necessary steps to electronic essay production. The instructional method used to teach musical instruments is simply carried over to the composition classroom. A keyboard is a keyboard, and there is a certain level of hand-eye coordination that must be established before a student is deemed proficient at that particular instrument he or she is playing, whether that instrument is a piano or a computer. Until that level of hand-eye coordination is achieved, the student will be anxious. This initial phase is critical in both piano instruction and computer instruction because the student may become so frustrated that he or she quits.

Awareness of this critical period in student computer instruction is the first step toward reducing electronic writing anxiety. As a result, orientation to the laboratory experience is a necessary step that enables my students to adapt to the equipment. The time spent in the lab performing various single objective lessons aids students in learning the routine of a particular lab setting. In general, if a student is comfortable in the environment, or feels at home, the level of anxiety is greatly reduced, allowing the "teachable moment" to occur. This "teachable moment" occurs in the lab on a regular basis because when students are permitted to explore the computer software, including Netscape to access the Internet, the students come to appreciate the power of the resources available to them by a simple click of the mouse button.

There is a caveat here for those students who click the wrong mouse button; however, that is the reason a facilitator must be present in the lab while students explore the software. A novice can become easily lost in cyberspace without an organized method of approach. Hence, I assign an Internet search as one of my lab assignments so my students will learn what all those icons mean. They learn by doing. The objective of the lesson is to develop their computer screen reading skills. In effect, they are developing their hand-eye coordination because they must use their hands to click the mouse button and press keys on the keyboard while they are looking at the computer screen to decide what to do next. They must read the entire computer screen at once, meaning they must read holistically. After a while, they learn to focus on specific areas of the screen because they learn where the icons for particular tasks are usually placed in the software.

In addition to learning how to read the screen, the students must discover which search engines are the most reliable and which information is credible. In fact, my students learn quickly that there is an abundance of poor quality information on the Internet as well as quality information. One objective of the Internet assignment is to distinguish between the two types of information. Another objective of the Internet assignment is to learn how to read all of the information on the Web sites. Essentially, reading is a large part of any Internet search to the extent that to be able to sort through all of those Web sites, an Internet user must be able to determine which links will be the most productive to his or her search. Training the eye to focus holistically on the screen, as opposed to a linear, left to right movement, enables the user to find appropriate information in a swifter manner.

In the final analysis, although we may express a desire to have all the latest equipment for our students, it may not be necessary to always have the top of the line, especially when it may sit idle because few can operate it. Essentially, computers should not be stored away like all of that exercise equipment purchased around New Year's Day with good intentions that never materialize. Just like Bic pens in the 1960s, computers have become the writing tools of today. They are the unavoidable writing tools of the global community. Unfortunately, not all members of the global community that has been created by computer technology are fully enfranchised because they do not have access to, or do not know how to operate, the very instruments that give them voice in that community. Without a voice in the discourse community of the Internet, a person cannot participate in the public discourse that, according to Berlin, is the avenue for "individuals working together . . . trying to decide what will be in the best interests of the group and the individual" (15). The issue still stands: Should the information superhighway provide public access to all members of the global community, or is it destined to become a toll road? Either way, the composition classroom is the on-ramp.

Work Cited

Berlin, James. *Rhetoric and Reality: Writing Instruction in American Colleges, 1990–1995*. Carbondale: Southern Illinois University Press, 1987.

Portfolios as a Part of the Developmental Writing Classroom

By PATRICIA I. MULCAHY-ERNT, Ph.D.
University of Bridgeport

As teachers of writing have changed the focus of their instruction from a product-orientation to a process-orientation, the attractiveness of portfolios as both an instructional tool and an assessment tool has increased in developmental writing classrooms. Deciding on the use of portfolios, however, is analogous to making a New Year's resolution for a complete body make-over: if you want good results, you cannot make a halfhearted effort; likewise, once you make the total commitment, you will see a substantial change not only in the outcome but in your everyday routines. So, if you are contemplating using portfolios, you may want to ask some critical questions. What is the best use of portfolios for my classrooms? How can I use portfolios for instruction as well as assessment of students' writing? What are some of the benefits as well as drawbacks in using portfolios?

Portfolios as a process approach

To begin, using portfolios for both instruction and assessment incorporates a process approach. In other words, the focus is on the development of students' writing in various stages and forms, rather than the finished product. Although one definition of portfolio use, common to artists and writers, is the collection of their best pieces, representing the expertise and versatility of the artist, the alternative and more widely used version of the portfolio in the developmental writing classroom is the collection of work over time, representing the student's growth as a writer. By definition, a portfolio is a systematic collection of student work (Valencia, 1991; Popham, 1995). As a collection of snapshots of student work, a portfolio has examples of a student's progress and achievement, showing how over time the student has changed and matured in different aspects of writing. These artifacts of student work constitute a representative sample of the depth and breadth of the student's performance.

Due to the link between a process approach to writing and the use of portfolios as snapshots of student work in the various phases of the writing process, portfolios have a natural niche in the developmental writing classroom. As an assessment tool, the instructor can evaluate the student's progress, based on the student's actual work situated in the actual writing contexts. In contrast to other forms of assessment, the power of portfolios is that they are considered authentic, especially in light of the writing tasks the students are requested to do and the context of instruction (Valencia, 1991). In other words, the tools for assessment are grounded in the same tasks that are used for instruction. Unlike other forms of assessments that are not aligned with instruction, portfolios are considered a more valid, naturalistic type of evaluation.

However, the worth of using portfolios is not just as an approach for evaluation but as an approach for instruction. The dynamic properties of a portfolio system emerge when an instructor adopts a portfolio approach for instruction. To do so, an instructor designs classroom instruction that allows for planning, drafting, conferencing, revision, reflection, and student choice, which are often part of a writing classroom. For example, not only does the student choose writing samples for inclusion in a folder of student work, but both the instructor and student participate in individual conferences to discuss the student's progress; records of these conferences are included in the student's portfolio. The student also participates in peer conferences; records of these conferences also become part of the portfolio. When the student revises a paper, the revision, especially in contrast to the original paper, is included in the portfolio. Throughout the semester, however, the student may decide to substitute a revised "best piece" after a series of revisions. Included in the portfolio may be the student's own writing reflections that promote a metacognitive awareness of the writing process and the student's own individual growth as a writer. Unlike more traditional types of assessment that depend on performance on one type of task, such as a multiple-choice test or essay test, a portfolio system approach relies on multiple measures gained through the processes of conferencing, revision, student choice, and self-reflection; the final grade includes these multiple measures of growth collected throughout an entire instructional period rather than a single score gained on one assessment given during a single-setting exam period.

Using portfolios as a process approach for both instruction and assessment contains a number of implicit assumptions about writing, instruction, the participation of students, the role of the writing instructor, and the role of assessment. First of all, the process of writing is linked to the other language arts processes; students learn how to improve their writing by sharing their ideas with others, discussing their writing, reading the work of others, and incorporating the feedback of peers and mentors in their own work. Second, assessment is aligned with instruction and shows the ongoing efforts of students in a variety of writing tasks and contexts; particularly for the field of writing, portfolios can indicate the planning, drafting, conferencing about, revising, and publishing of a student's piece of writing. Rarely is this process captured in other evaluation tools. Third, students as writers and readers become part of the process of writing instruction along with the instructor; since peer feedback helps students learn about writing to communicate to an audience, the peer conference summaries can also be included in the portfolio. Due to this emphasis, writing becomes a social, collaborative activity, rather than an isolated, solely independent one. In this sense, students are stakeholders in the instruction-assessment process, unlike more traditional formats. Fourth, the role of the writing instructor shifts to that of a mentor, a coach, a trusted confidante. The feedback that the student receives, as well as the manner in which it is communicated to the student, can make a significant difference in building a student's self-confidence in writing ability; it can motivate a student to take risks, to try new styles and patterns, to view another's writing in a new light. Therefore, individual conferences between the student and instructor become part of both the instructional as well as assessment approach. However, evaluation of a student's work is formative, focusing on the emergence and process of the writer. Often, instructors using a portfolio approach will write descriptive notes about a student's performance so that the student's writing strengths are also noted as well as areas for improvement; or, conference notes may be specific to a focused area for development, such as writing for a stylistic effect. The instructor's role also shifts from a traditional classroom lecturer to one that requires redesigning the classroom for peer discussion, for the use of writing tools for revision, and for collaboration among teachers and students. Finally, if portfolios are implemented in a writing program across a series of courses, careful planning among administrators and instructors needs to occur so that decisions about the contents of the portfolio, the assessment of the portfolio as a whole, and the final ownership of the portfolio are made before portfolios are used for the whole curriculum.

Decisions about using portfolios for instruction and assessment

In a developmental writing classroom the integration of a portfolio system depends on three key stages: planning, implementation, and evaluation. During the phase in which the instructor plans to use a portfolio system, several key decisions about the purpose of the portfolio, the contents of the portfolio, and the ownership of the portfolio need to be made.

Purpose

In any good assessment approach the purpose of testing and evaluation needs to be clear. In other words, what needs to be evaluated? Why? Typically, the case for the inclusion of portfolios in a developmental writing classroom is that they show the student's growth in writing over time; samples of the student's own writing are the focus for both instruction and assessment. Hopefully, the purpose of testing and evaluation are in alignment with instruction. In other words, the benefit of using portfolios is that the processes of planning, drafting, conferencing, and revision are exemplified in both instruction and assessment.

Contents

Deciding about the contents of the portfolio has important effects not only for instruction but also for assessment. The definition of the portfolio as a folder of the student's best pieces warrants a selective process in weeding out writings that the student no longer considers "best"; this focus keeps to a minimum the number of pieces that are included. In contrast, if the definition of a portfolio is to include a process perspective, showing how the student creates the "best pieces," then the quantity of items will be greater. In the latter case students will include examples of their planning, drafting, conferencing, and revising.

In a developmental writing classroom there are many feasible items for inclusion in a portfolio. Some of the more popular types of items are the following:

- Selected best pieces;
- Samples of different types of writing, such as narrative, expository, persuasive pieces; poetry; autobiographical pieces; letters; résumé;
- Examples of drafts, revisions, and edited manuscripts;
- Conference notes from both peer and teacher-student conferences;
- Self-evaluation summaries of the student's writing.

Since portfolios can be shaped to the contours of the writing classroom, depending on the types of writing tasks used, portfolios can include a variety of other representative works. If a student is involved in an in-depth research project, the writing portfolio could include samples of the student's field notes, such as personal interviews, observations, journal entries, outlines, and library research summaries. Portfolios also allow the use of multiple texts in various formats. For instance, depending on the writing task, portfolios can include works on computer, on videotape, in photographs, and in other media. This quality of portfolios provides a creative appeal to instructors who wish to provide an incentive to students to apply what they write to performance settings, such as a play.

In classrooms that focus on both developmental reading and writing, the portfolio can include students' responses to text, study notes, and vocabulary notes. Also, a portfolio can provide evidence how the student is applying literacy strategies in other classes; in other words, samples that show how the student is comprehending text and studying other disciplines may also be included in the portfolio to show how the student transfers acquired skills in the developmental classroom to other disciplines.

If the portfolio is used for long-range assessment, it may also include other types of tests that serve to provide normative data about the student's performance in relation to other students' performance. For instance, it is a widespread practice in many colleges to give students a writing test, typically for placement purposes. Therefore, as a baseline measure of writing performance, the student's writing test could also be included in the portfolio. Since students in developmental writing classes typically take a series of writing courses, then the student's portfolio could also travel with the student through those courses. Any final writing exams required by the college could also be placed in the student's portfolio. In other words, if a portfolio approach is adopted as a departmental policy for student evaluation, then the writing that the student completes during participation in a writing program can be evaluated through a long-range process. The benefit of this systems approach for evaluating students' writing is that there is naturalistic evidence of the student's progress and multiple measures of writing achievement. Thus, when portfolios are used to evaluate the student's writing through an entire program, rather than a single course, portfolios may include standardized test results to indicate performance in a variety of contexts. However, the inclusion of items in a portfolio, whether they are standardized test results or measures of naturalistic writing samples, should have a clear rationale in alignment with the goals of writing instruction.

Ownership

One of the attractions of a portfolio approach is that students take ownership for the contents of it, thereby having a voice in their own evaluation; through the process of selecting what is included in the portfolio, students are actively involved in both their instruction and assessment. Without a doubt, a portfolio is a testimony to a student's diligence, especially in the revision process, and the pride that the student takes in the creation of a portfolio is an important dimension in its success. However, since the portfolio collects evidence over time, it is often feasible to keep the physical folder and a copy of the student's work in the developmental writing classroom or writing lab so that the evidence is not lost. Yet, it is also important that the student has a personal copy of all of the portfolio works, has access to the portfolio, and has the authority to choose and discard work that is no longer characterized as best pieces. At the same time security for the contents of the portfolio needs to be maintained so that only the owner of the portfolio has access to it and that any standardized test scores are not lost.

To preserve the integrity of ownership of the portfolio, some instructors will hold an initial conference with the student to create a contract about the types of items the student will include (such as writing samples), the types of items that the instructor will include (such as conference notes), and the types of items the department will include (such as standardized tests or department writing tests). In this manner it is clear at the beginning of the semester who is responsible for completing and maintaining the various components of the portfolio. In some cases the student maintains complete control over the portfolio and is responsible for turning in the finished portfolio at the end of the semester.

Implementation

The implementation stage of using portfolios spans both classroom instruction and assessment. After the decision about where to physically keep the student folders is made and after the initial contract is negotiated with the student, the instructor uses the portfolio as a bank of the students' writings. Since the advantage of using portfolios is that they align with the natural flow in a writing classroom, the instructor can recommend that students include in their portfolios samples portraying their writing process.

However, one feature of portfolios that complements good writing instruction is the inclusion of instructor-student and peer conferences. Included in the portfolio can be samples that indicate an awareness of audience, style, tone, appropriateness, organization, voice, word choice (Tierney, Carter, & Desai, 1991); the effectiveness of each of these can be discussed through conferences. As a record of the conference, the instructor can design a checklist and summary sheet, noting the student's strengths and areas for improvement. (See Tierney, Carter, & Desai, 1991 for examples of checklists.)

Evaluation

The last phase of portfolio use entails evaluation. If the instructor has already clear-cut goals for instruction, then the assessment process should be in alignment. However, the challenge of portfolio assessment is to decide on what should be evaluated. The well-stocked portfolio has an enormous amount of data. One evaluation approach is to use holistic grading on the quality of the entire contents. A recommendation is to develop a rubric that clearly spells out different ranges of quality. In other words, what is an outstanding portfolio? Acceptable one? Weak one? Unacceptable one? Characteristics for each of these descriptors need to be clearly identified and communicated to the student during the instructional process. (See Tierney, Carter, & Desai, 1991 for examples of rubrics.)

Hopefully, the final portfolio grade is also part of formative evaluation. Since the student receives feedback about the writing samples created for the classroom (which are included in the portfolio), the final evaluation should be no surprise. Yet, in the spirit of consistency and collaboration the final portfolio evaluation should include solid descriptors of the student's performance. In this manner the student is able to learn how to improve writing performance.

Challenges in using portfolios

The astute reader will note that the implementation of a portfolio system is no small matter in the classroom. There are a number of challenges and drawbacks to portfolio use, among them are time, adequate resources, the availability of professional training, and the reliability of evaluation results.

Time

First, it takes not only a substantial commitment to using portfolios, but it also takes much time to develop a workable system for the classroom and even longer for a whole department. Some instructors have adopted a two-year plan for the development of their systems: the first year is to create the initial design and make a trial run of the use of portfolios, and the second year is to fine-tune the process.

Adequate resources

Secondly, portfolios need a physical space to house their contents. A well-organized, accessible, and secure area, which should be in the proximity of the writing classroom, needs to be created. Student folders need to be purchased, some type of filing system needs to be created, and the physical storage of the portfolios needs to be available. Although this may not seem like a challenge to those working with small populations, in some colleges involving the participation of hundreds of students in freshman writing programs, this is no small matter. The alternative is for students to be responsible for their own portfolios.

Availability of professional training

In order for a portfolio system to work, instructors, administrators, and students, must be well-versed in those aspects influencing their role in the planning, implementation, and evaluation of portfolios. For example, instructors need to know how to design them for their own classrooms, how to create the appropriate instructional tools for student use, and how to evaluate their contents. Department administrators need to be aware of the commitment in time and resources that instructors and students make in creating a viable portfolio system. Also, students need to learn how to develop their portfolio, participate in its evaluation, and become part of a team of peer evaluators.

Reliability of evaluation results

Finally, as an assessment tool, the reliability of portfolios has been called into question (Popham, 1995). Psychometrically speaking, for a test to be reliable, it needs to give consistent results. Unlike standardized measures that are designed to give consistent, stable results, portfolios lack consistency. In other words, different evaluators can assign different grades. This is a concern among those who use portfolios; often the articulation of clear criteria for grading the contents of the portfolio has been cited as a first step in addressing this concern. However, without good training in evaluating writing and in evaluating portfolios, the merits of using a portfolio system are minimized.

In sum, as you decide on the worth of portfolios for your classroom, you are now in a better position to stick to your resolution, unlike making a New Year's resolution born out of guilt rather than felt need. Hopefully, as means to an end, your students will also enjoy the process and the outcome of your instructional decision-making, whatever you decide.

Recommended readings

deFina, A. A. (1992). *Portfolio assessment: Getting started.* New York: Scholastic.

Farr, R. & Tone, B. (1994). *Portfolio and performance assessment.* Fort Worth: Harcourt Brace.

Gillett, J. W. & Temple, C. (1994). *Understanding reading problems: Assessment & instruction, 4th edition.* New York: HarperCollins.

Harp, B. (1996). *The handbook of literacy assessment and evaluation.* Norwood, MA: Christopher-Gordon.

Johnston, P. H. (1992). *Constructive evaluation of literate activity.* New York: Longman.

Popham, W. J. (1995). *Classroom assessment: What teachers need to know.* Boston: Allyn & Bacon.

Roskos, K. & Walker, B. J. (1994). *Interactive handbook for understanding reading diagnosis.* New York: Merrill.

Tierney, R. J., Carter, M. A., Desai, L. E. (1991). *Portfolio assessment in the reading-writing classroom.* Norwood, MA: Christopher-Gordon.

Valencia, S. W. (1991). Portfolios: Panacea or Pandora's Box? In F. L. Finch (ed.), *Educational performance assessment* (pp. 33–46). Chicago: Riverside.

Electronic Portfolios in ESL Writing: An Alternative Approach

By SAAD AL KAHTANI
Indiana University of Pennsylvania

1. Introduction

Electronic writing portfolios are computer-based learning media. They have been introduced to English classes in the late twentieth century (Hawisher & Self, 1997). Among the many purposes they were created for is conducting formative and summative assessments of student learning. This new medium has hypertext capability, which Charney (1994) believes will "change fundamentally how we write, how we read, how we teach these skills, and even how we conceive of text itself" (p. 239).

Teachers in many schools and universities are beginning to ask their students to put their written work on the Web as electronic projects rather than in the traditional essay format. Warschauer and Healey (1998) predict that the paper essay may become a "marked form" in the next 10 to 20 years. That is, most written documents will be composed electronically rather than on paper. In response to this situation, they suggest that English as a Second Language (ESL) teachers will need to instruct their students to have their writing on the Web and to use the Internet not as a "distribution medium" but as a medium in its own right. This, in their view, is fitting for the multimedia environment, where students will want to combine a variety of media—text, graphics, sounds, videos and images—without losing the big picture, which is the language learning.

2. What is a portfolio?

Although the definition of *portfolio* may vary, for the purpose of this discussion a portfolio is "a systematic and selective collection of student work that has been assembled to demonstrate the student's motivation, academic growth, and level of achievement" (Norton & Wiburg, 1998, p. 237). Freeman and Freeman (1994) define a portfolio as a "box or a folder which contains various kinds of information that has been gathered over time about one student" (p. 259). Their definition of a portfolio goes on to include recorded information of a student's work on an audiotape or videotape. For this, students videotape or audiotape the process of their projects and include them with other materials in their portfolios.

Two common types of portfolio are a work portfolio, where students keep their works in progress, and a showcase portfolio, where students highlight their best work in ways that show their development and growth.

3. What is an electronic portfolio?

An electronic portfolio is a purposeful collection of a student's work that is made available on the World Wide Web or a recordable CD-ROM. It is similar to the traditional portfolio that consists of papers and folders; however, the medium this portfolio uses is different. It uses a combination of electronic media such as hypermedia programs, databases, spreadsheets, and word-processing software, as well as CD-ROMs and the Web. The electronic portfolio can be print-based, saved on a computer disk, compiled on a CD-ROM or Web homepage, or a combination of the above. The information can take the form of text, graphics, videos, sounds, images, or any other multimedia format. Although print documents may be included in this kind of portfolio, the electronic portfolio can take other forms: completely electronic, multiple formed (documents and electronic), and multiple linear (hypertextual) (Yancey & Weiser, 1997).

4. Why create and use electronic portfolios in ESL classrooms?

There are a number of advantages in creating electronic portfolios to be used in ESL writing classrooms. In the past, it was difficult and time consuming to locate students' folders stored in compartments or other places for safe keeping. The electronic portfolio is easier for both teachers and students to access electronically and retrieve all the information they need.

Another advantage of the electronic portfolio is the amount of space it takes relative to the traditional one. For paper portfolios, students need thick three-ring binders to hold the work they collect over a period of time, such as pictures, cassettes, videotapes, samples of writing, and so on. With electronic portfolios, the same information can be collected, stored and managed electronically, taking very little or no physical space. All of the portfolios for an entire class may be stored without having any space problems. At the end of the year or semester, students can have their work saved on floppy disks or burned onto a recordable CD-ROM, a compact disk that can store up to 650 MB of information (equivalent to 300,000 sheets of typed text).

Electronic portfolios may also be used for teacher planning. Teachers can acquire information about students in incoming classes from an existing portfolio system to plan for the coming school year. Allen et al. (1997) pointed out that a group of post-secondary teacher-researchers (PORTNET) across the United States were able to exchange their own portfolios over the Internet for discussion and evaluation. The same thing can be done with students' portfolios to find out about their levels and abilities before teaching them. This can happen by trading students' existing portfolio Web addresses (URLs) using electronic mail. A teacher can then access the portfolio by going to that Web address.

Although motivation is an abstract thing, displaying students' work on the Web is a significant motivating aspect for students, which they don't get when producing their work only for the teacher. To support this claim, Frizler (1995) suggests that students do better in writing when they know that they are going public and writing for a much wider audience that extends beyond the classroom and school boundaries. He further suggests that having students use the Web as a medium to present their portfolio will make them feel as if their work is published. Confirming this view is Phinney (1996), who states that her students have the option of producing electronic papers using a toolbook (programming software) application, which includes digitized sound, video and still images, to present their arguments instead of writing a traditional paper. Although the mechanics were often more difficult, the students who chose to do the electronic paper "enjoyed it immensely." Many appeared to be more involved in their work and produced interesting hypertexts.

Like most information on the Web, the content and organization of electronic portfolios can be upgraded and periodically updated. Students can always access their work on the Web using their passwords. They can change or add documentation that best represents their learning and growth.

5. Content of the electronic portfolio

Teachers and their students need to discuss the content of the electronic portfolios at the beginning of the semester. This discussion would give students ideas about what to include in their portfolios but would not prespecify the content. The content could include students' work, peer response forms, teachers' comments and feedback, and reading journals, as well as other items.

5.1 Students' work

Students may include any work they have done for the course as long as they have a purpose for that work to be included. Their essays, for example, can be included, using subtitles to represent the sequence (e.g., Essay #1, #2, #3, etc.). To help students learn how to transfer their work onto the Web, the teacher may ask them to bring their essays saved on diskettes and then teach them how to upload those essays. In this way, the students receive instruction about the process using their own essays. Students can be advised to use the potential of hypertext or hypermedia to support their essay arguments. For example, if they are writing about celebrating Martin Luther King, Jr.'s birthday, they can link to another essay on the Internet that talks about the same event or they can import a video clip that contains King's "I have a Dream" speech. Students can also use pictures or images to support or illustrate a statement or argument in their writing.

5.2 Peer response forms

With each student's essay it is helpful to have a peer response form which peers use to respond to their classmates' essays. This electronic peer response form can include questions that students answer when responding to their peers' writing. The following are examples of questions that can be attached to the electronic peer response form:

What is the strongest part of this writing?

What are your suggestions for revision?

What questions do you have for the author?

After writing their responses, students can press the button "Submit" to send their responses directly to the essay author. (See Figure 1.)

5.3 Teachers' comments and feedback

With each student's essay there can be a "Mail to" link for the teacher's feedback. The teacher can use that link or form to send students' comments and feedback. The feedback can be sent directly to the student's e-mail account or can stay in the student's electronic portfolio. Students will have to check to view the

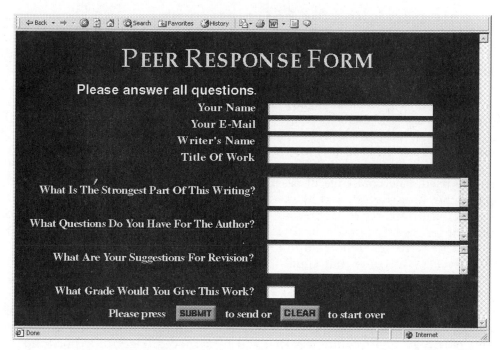

For more details, see http://www.iup.edu/~nickm/peer.htm

Figure 1. Electronic peer response form.

feedback on a regular basis. Sending feedback directly to the student's e-mail account would ensure the privacy of feedback; however, students may delete them accidentally without reading them or mix them up with other messages. The other option (keeping them on the electronic portfolio) would ease retrieving them at any time, yet the main drawback is that feedback and comments can be viewed by other students (Almozainy, 1997).

5.4 Reading journals

ESL writing teachers can assign students to write weekly journals about materials they have read during that week. They might also include a hypertext link to lead people interested in reading the original article. Their reflection can take the form of what they liked or disliked about the article, a review of the content, or even a summary of the article.

5.5 Miscellaneous

This last section on students' electronic portfolios may contain things that were not covered by the other section. To emphasize students' creativity, the teacher may leave the content of this section entirely up to the students to put in whatever they think is relevant to their learning, such as pictures, sounds, movies, or any other materials. There should be no limitation as to what is put in this section. The only requirement the teacher might assign is for the students to write a short paragraph before each of the entries, describing why they selected it and how it helped them in learning to write in English (Almozainy, 1997).

6. Creating electronic portfolios for ESL classrooms

To create an electronic portfolio successfully, ESL writing teachers and their students need to look at several considerations.

The first point to be considered is that students must be computer literate and accustomed to the general appearance of Web pages. The teacher must be familiar with the hypertext markup language (HTML), have access to a number of computers equipped with programs that can be used in creating electronic portfolios, and be willing to work with technology. (See Figure 2.)

The second consideration is the context in which the electronic portfolio will be used. The challenge of creating electronic portfolios is that traditional approaches are still followed by many ESL writing teachers. Although some ESL teachers and researchers appreciate the process approach, product proponents still call for focusing on form, since what will be evaluated is the final product of student writing. Some compromising voices, such as that of Fathman and Whalley (1990), stress that equal focus should be given to both product and process. To utilize the full potential of electronic portfolios, ESL teachers should not stick to traditional ways of teaching writing.

The third aspect to be considered is the purpose of creating a portfolio. Teachers and students should never create a portfolio without a clear goal for their portfolios and the progress that can be achieved. Electronic portfolios are not meant to include everything a student produces. Therefore, students and teachers should have criteria for what they are going to display in their portfolios before they start creating them.

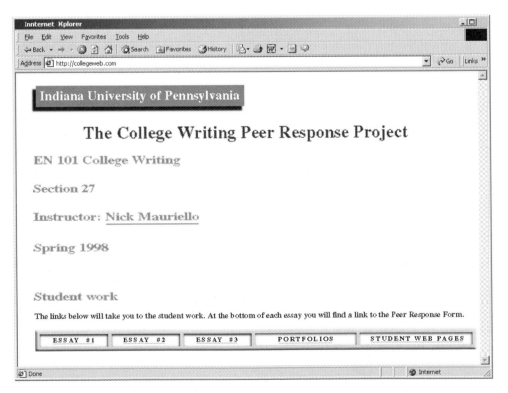

Source: Pagnucci & Mauriello's Fall 1998 College Writing Peer Response Project

Figure 2. An example of electronic writing portfolio.

A final consideration is the organization of the electronic portfolio. Although there is no one way of organizing electronic portfolios, they should be organized to give an accurate picture of the student's development. The main menu of an electronic portfolio can be organized around a set of buttons that represent both the student's and the teacher's visions of what is important to include and what the audience may value.

7. Tools for creating electronic portfolios

One or more of the following items of software and hardware can be used to create an electronic portfolio.

Software	Hardware
1. Pro View 2.1 E-magine Software Inc.	A legal-size flatbed scanner (minimum 8.5″ by 11.66″)
2. Hyperstudio Roger Wagner Publishing	A hand-held digital video camera
3. Word Processing Web Authoring (MS Word 97/2000)	

8. Conclusion

Creating electronic portfolios is a new trend in teaching languages in general and in teaching ESL writing in particular. They have several advantages over traditional portfolios that contain folders, papers, cassettes, videotapes, and more. Among the advantages of this type of portfolio are that information can be stored digitally on a computer hard drive or some sort of movable medium (floppy disk, zip disk, CD, etc.), it takes up very little space, and it can be easily accessed from anywhere and at any time when compatible equipment is available.

Despite the advantages, however, this type of portfolio has serious limitations. Two major limitations are that it can be used only by technologically literate students and it can be used only when the necessary equipment and software are available. With this level of technology, some students, especially those with low proficiency in computer skills, find it difficult to stay motivated, perceiving the virtual classroom as a hindrance to learning more than a benefit (Frizler, 1995). Technical problems that might occur, such as power failure and telephone line disconnections, are drawbacks to this type of technology. Another important disadvantage is that students may spend too much time on organizing their portfolios to make them look good in terms of graphics and design and pay less attention to the writing content. By the same token, teachers may find themselves teaching computer skills instead of writing.

Finally, and speaking from a whole language philosophy, students and teachers using this kind of technology should use it for enhancing the learning of composition and provide caution against its misuse. They should be aware of some of the software and look at how software technology views language learning.

References

Allen, M., Condon, W., Dickson, M., Forbes, C., Meese, G. & Yancey, K. (1997) "Portfolios, WAC, Email and assessment: An inquiry on PORTNET," in K. Yancey & I. Weiser (eds.) *Situating Portfolios: Four Perspectives*. Logan, UT: Utah State University Press, pp. 370–84.

Almozainy, Y. (1997) "Virtual portfolio: A learning tool for ESL writers." Paper presented at the Three Rivers TESOL, Morgantown, WV, November 1997.

Charney, D. (1994) "The effect of hypertext on processes of reading and writing," in C. Selfe & S. Hilligoss (eds.) *Literacy and Computers: The Complications of Teaching and Learning with Technology*. New York: Modern Language Association of America, pp. 238–63.

Fathman, A. & Whalley, E. (1990) "Teacher response to student writing: Focus on form versus content," in B. Krool (ed.) *Second Language Writing: Research Insights for the Classroom*. New York: Cambridge University Press, pp. 178–90.

Freeman, D. & Freeman, Y. (1994) *Whole Language Principles for Bilingual Learning: Under the Whole Language Umbrella*. Urban, IL: National Council of Teachers of English.

Frizler, K. (1995) *The Internet as an Educational Tool in ESOL Writing Instruction*. Unpublished M.A. thesis, San Francisco State University. Available online: *http://thecity.sfsu.edu/~funweb/thesis.htm*

Hawisher, G. & Self, C. (1997) "Wedding the technologies of writing portfolios and computers," in K. Yancey & I. Weiser (eds.) *Situating Portfolios: Four Perspectives*. Logan, UT: Utah State University Press, pp. 305–21.

Milone, M. (1995) "Electronic portfolios: Who's doing them and how?," *Technology and Learning* 16 (2): 28–33.

Norton, P. & Wiburg, K. (1998) *Teaching with Technology*. Orlando: Harcourt Brace College Publishers.

Phinney, M. (1996) "Exploring the virtual world: Computers in the second language writing classroom," in M. Pennington (ed.) *The Power of CALL*. Houston: Athelstan, pp. 137–52.

Warschauer, M. & Healey, D. (1998) "Computers and language learning," *Language Teaching* 3 (2): 57–71.

Yancey, K. & Weiser, I. (1997) "Situating portfolios: An introduction," in K. Yancey & I. Weiser (eds.) *Situating Portfolios: Four Perspectives*. Logan, UT: Utah State University Press, pp. 1–17.

Using Tutors in a Developmental Writing Class

By KARAN HANCOCK
and TOM GIER
University of Alaska—Anchorage

What is a tutor?

This seems to be a fairly straightforward question. A tutor is a person who has particular skill, expertise, or knowledge in a specific subject, content area, or discipline and who shares that skill, expertise, or knowledge with students one to one or in a group situation. Simply put, the goal of a tutor is to enable the person being tutored (the tutee) to acquire enough of the tutor's skills and expertise to become academically independent.

Why are tutors a valuable resource in the class and the writing lab?

A tutor can be a tremendous resource because a tutor can do what the professor many times cannot do: give the student absolute undivided attention for an extended period of time and repeat, explain, define, and reexplain material or information when necessary. A tutor can lead a student through an assignment or a project step by step and point by point and then do it again if necessary.

Tutors are a valuable resource. Often a student experiencing difficulty will be more likely to seek help when needed if tutors are available. What student has not been just a little frightened of calling on a professor during office hours or before or after class to ask about an assignment that everyone else in class seems to understand? Many students find they are much more comfortable approaching a fellow student—a tutor—with a problem or concern.

Well-trained tutors seem to have a special knack for helping these students, too. Maybe it is just because the tutor is "closer" to the assignment or project—the tutor can probably very quickly remember and share his/her own difficulties with the same or similar assignment and thereby help take some of the stigma away by simply saying: "Yeah, I had trouble with this, too," or "I can see where you're having some difficulty."

What else can tutors do either in the class or the writing lab? The following are some general "tutoring do's." By no means is the list complete because every class, writing lab, and tutoring situation will have particular issues that cannot be delineated or anticipated. However, the list will give tutors, students (tutees), and professors a starting point.

Tutoring "Do's"

How can a well-trained tutor help in the class and/or writing lab? What are some of the things a tutor does?

1. A tutor appreciates and respects the uniqueness of each individual student and realizes that every tutee has strengths and weaknesses.

2. A tutor helps the tutee identify areas of strength. This gives both a good place to start. By identifying what the student already knows or can do, the tutor can more easily pinpoint and address any weaknesses.

3. A tutor and the tutee next identify and address areas of weakness. If the student has difficulty with time management, it is going to be a waste of time to address topic sentences first. With the help of the tutee a tutor will be able to identify these areas of difficulty and then offer positive suggestions about how to best deal with them.

4. A tutor asks appropriate questions that help the tutee identify just where the difficulty lies. "What do you understand the assignment to be? Explain it to me as you understand it." By ascertaining the tutee's level of understanding of the assignment, the tutor can then take the questioning further.
   Some additional questions might include:

   "What can you do with the assignment right now?"

   "What skills do you have that you can use to begin this assignment?"

   "What skills do you think you need to review or sharpen before you can begin this assignment?"

   "What is typically the first thing you do when approaching an assignment?"

   "What is the most difficult thing for you about this assignment?"

   "What is the least difficult?"

   "How much time are you going to allot for the assignment?"

   "Having talked about your difficulties, do you think this is going to be enough time?"

   Answers the tutee provides to these and other questions will give the tutor a specific place to start and help him/her plan appropriately.

5. A tutor makes diagnoses based on the information gleaned from the tutee and goes on to help the tutee overcome the identified areas of weakness while expanding on areas of strength. For example, if time management is identified as a problem area, maybe all that is needed is a review of the student's master schedule to help her/him see which pieces or blocks of time can be devoted to a specific class or assignment. If the initial discussion reveals that the tutee needs help in narrowing a topic then the work can begin there with a specific goal in mind. The tutee can then use the same questioning techniques to self-diagnose for other classes and other assignments.

6. The tutor helps the tutee establish a positive attitude about a class or assignment. Some students do poorly in a class or on an assignment because they have no real interest in it or cannot see the relevance of it. The class or assignment is just something they have to get through. The tutee may never really come to "love" writing a research paper; but through the help of a tutor, a tutee may come to appreciate the process and why it was assigned.

7. A tutor helps to foster positive self-esteem in the tutee. By helping the tutee acquire or polish skills and set reasonable, attainable goals, the tutor is helping the tutee learn to take charge and take responsibility for his/her own learning and academic success.

8. A tutor expresses empathy, understanding, and respect for the tutee's difficulty. If a student has been away from the academic world for a while or is new to the college/university setting, the tutor may need to start with dusting off long-unused "student skills" or even introduce the student to new student skills. A tutor may need to demonstrate how to use the computer that now takes the place of the card catalog in the library; which version of documentation style, MLA or APA, etc. is now required; how to format a computer for proper margins, etc.

   A tutor may need to start by helping the tutee with very basic writing techniques: outlining, narrowing a topic, broadening a topic, political correctness in writing, subject-verb agreement, pronoun-antecedent agreement, parallelism, imagery, etc. With some students/tutees, it may be necessary to start with basic vocabulary skills, sentence structure, grammar, and punctuation. Within the class or writing lab, a tutor helps students recognize and address these types of difficulties.

9. A tutor shares with the tutee a variety of examples and techniques. Within the writing lab, a tutor can refer to any number of "process papers" to show the student exactly what is meant and expected by a particular professor. (It is especially helpful when the professor and tutor work together to have a file of examples to share with the tutee. These papers can exemplify just what the professor expects in a particular type of assignment.)

10. A tutor listens to what the tutee has to say and responds appropriately. Sometimes all a tutee needs is an opportunity to "talk through" a problem area or difficulty with someone else. Sometimes a tutee needs very specific help and can very succinctly ask for it; sometimes not. Sometimes a tutee needs a little pat on the back and a nod of encouragement. Sometimes the tutee comes to the tutoring session wanting help that the tutor is not able to provide; therefore, an effective tutor knows when and to whom the tutee should be referred.

This is a beginning list of some basic "Tutoring Do's." Each tutor working with the professor and writing lab should establish additional points as they specifically apply to their individual programs, settings, and students.

Tutoring "Don'ts"

It is important for tutors, professors, and tutees to realize that there are some things that do not fall into the scope of tutoring. As with the list of "Tutoring Do's," this list of general "Tutoring Don'ts" is just a beginning that can be expanded upon to fit the needs of the particular situation.

1. A tutor does not do the work for the tutee. A tutor's job is to help the student understand, begin, progress through, and complete the assignment. A tutor is NOT a ghost writer and does not do the assignment for the student.

2. A tutor does not tell the student how easy an assignment is or should be. Just because an assignment seems easy or self-explanatory to the tutor does not mean the tutee finds it so. If the assignment were easy why would the

student be seeking help from a tutor? A tutor never belittles the difficulty a tutee may be having.

3. A tutor does not assume the role of a counselor. The tutor's role is academic, not psychological. Tutors are not trained counselors or therapists. This does not mean that a tutor cannot listen to a nonacademic problem—what it does mean is that a tutor should know when and to whom the student may be referred for appropriate help.

4. A tutor does not let the tutoring extend past the point of necessity. Some tutees seem absolutely unable to work on their own and seek continued tutoring when it really isn't necessary. An effective tutor will have given the tutee the skills and practice necessary to progress on his/her own and the independence to do so. If the tutee insists that the tutor is "the only one who can help me" or "I can't do it without you" then there may be a need for intervention by the writing lab supervisor or the professor.

5. A tutor does not take on tutees with whom he/she cannot be comfortable. If a tutor is not comfortable working with much older students, very young students, or any student with whom rapport cannot be easily established, then the tutor owes it to himself or herself and the tutee to realize that and recommend another tutor.

   An addendum to this is the tutor does not become personally involved with the tutee. It is crucial to maintain professionalism in the tutoring situation. There should be prescribed places to meet for the tutoring sessions, i.e., the writing lab, the classroom, or the resource center.

6. A tutor does not predict grades on projects or assignments.

7. A tutor does not criticize a professor's assignments, how assignments are graded, how a professor presents material, or how a professor tests. A tutor will help the student understand the grading criteria, assignments, etc. of professors and encourage the student to visit with the professor to go over the errors and shortcomings.

8. A tutor does not "fake" knowledge or expertise that he/she does not have. It is better to say, "I don't know that. Let's work on it together to find out" than to bluff one's way through something. This provides good modeling for the tutees by showing them that when tutors don't know an answer, they look it up.

9. A tutor remembers to praise the tutee and offer positive reinforcement and encouragement. The smallest step forward is just that: a step forward.

10. A tutor does not conduct the tutoring session as a one-way experience with information, directives, comments, and ideas coming only from the tutor. The successful tutoring session will be a two-way, give-and-take experience in which the tutor encourages questions, comments, and input from the tutee and expresses appreciation for the tutee's active involvement.

Responsibilities and qualities of a tutor

As with any job there are specific responsibilities and qualities that make the job and the person doing the job special. It is a given that the tutor will have the content area or discipline expertise that qualifies him/her to be a tutor in the first place and the tutor will have the desire to share that with the tutees.

But having expertise and desire are only part of the equation. A successful tutor also has special qualities and responsibilities that must be factored in as well.

As with the lists of tutoring do's and don'ts, this is just a beginning list and the tutors, professors, and writing lab supervisors will want to add to and adapt it to meet their own special needs. What follows are some basic tutor responsibilities and qualities.

1. A tutor is ready before the tutoring session begins. If the tutoring is done in the classroom, the tutor must know what the topic of the day is, what is going to be covered, how it is going to be covered and what is going to be assigned from it. The tutor must then work closely with the professor to ensure that they are both "on the same page."

If the tutoring is taking place in the writing lab, the tutor must be there before the tutoring session starts in order to get physically and mentally ready for the session: reviewing notes, texts, reference materials and getting the space ready for the tutee and the ensuing session. If the tutor has worked with a particular tutee before, the tutor should be ready to discuss and review the last session's work and the progress and/or difficulties the tutee has had since the last meeting.

If the tutor is working with a tutee for the first time, the tutor must be ready to ask appropriate questions to help diagnose the tutee's areas of concern or difficulty. The main responsibility of a first session is to establish positive rapport with the tutee.

How is this done? A tutor should greet her/his tutee with friendliness and a smile. Remember, the tutee is probably more than a little nervous! Don't just jump right into tutoring. Begin by asking the tutee's name, what other classes he/she is taking, etc.—in other words, make some brief small talk. But also keep in mind that this is a working session, not a social session.

The tutor then asks the tutee to describe as specifically as possible the area(s) of concern or difficulty, using appropriate questioning skills, not interrogation. The tutor is advised to take notes about what the tutee is saying. In fact, it is a good idea for tutors to keep a file or reference sheet for each tutee. This file could be as simple or as complex as the tutor wishes to make it. Some things to include would be: the tutee's name, class he/she is seeking help with, what the specific areas of difficulty are, what diagnoses the tutor makes, and what the tutor prescribes be done in as much detail as possible. It is also important to note what the tutee is going to do before the next session and detail what the tutee will bring to the next tutoring session. Of course, the tutor goes over these notes with the tutee to make sure the information is complete, accurate, and understood.

2. The tutor should make sure that both the tutor and the tutee ask questions and make comments as the sessions progress. It is not a one-way communication process. The tutor asks questions and explains and the tutee must be encouraged to do the same. Some tutees may be a little reluctant at first to join in the dialogue for any number of reasons, ranging from it not being the custom in their culture to being shy or embarrassed. If the tutee is reluctant, the tutor may help open the dialogue by asking the tutee to now explain the process back to him/her, to "teach" the tutor, or to summarize the session.

3. Tutors must be willing to take the sessions one step at a time and one thing at a time and not rush through or assume the tutee has specific knowledge. An entire essay cannot be written in one tutoring session, but the tutor can help the tutee write a good outline or topic sentence.

4. Tutors must know when to "sit back and be quiet!" Rapid-fire questions or instructions are not going to help the tutor or the tutee. It is the responsibility of the effective tutor to give the tutee "time to think through" an answer, idea, or instruction. An effective tutor realizes that silence can be an effective tutoring tool and understands when to use it.

5. At the end of the tutoring session, don't just say, "Well, time's up. See you next time." The tutor should take time to summarize what was done and accomplished during the session. A good way to do this is to ask the tutee to comment on or summarize the session. (This can be a way to draw out the tutee who is reluctant to talk.) Be sure to jot these comments down on the tutee's reference sheet taking time to detail what the tutee will do or prepare for the next session. Again, make notes of what is discussed so that both tutor and tutee know and are in agreement. Make sure to end the session on a positive note by praising the tutee on his/her hard work and progress.

Other qualities of effective tutors:

1. patient
2. empathic, supportive, and nonjudgmental
3. resourceful and flexible
4. respectful of differences

Responsibilities and qualities of the tutee

What are some of the qualities and responsibilities of the tutees? These are very important to the ultimate success of the tutor/tutee relationship and should be discussed at the first session. Tutees must be aware of their role in the class and in the tutoring session and that they are responsible for their subsequent academic success or failure.

1. Tutees must attend all class meetings. It is the tutee's responsibility to "acquire" the material in the first place. A tutor cannot possibly help if the tutee comes to the session saying: "I missed class the other day, so I don't know what we're supposed to do." This is especially crucial if the tutor is in the writing lab and not present in the class. If this is the case, the tutor should point out to the tutee that it is the tutee's responsibility to attend class, to be aware of what is assigned, due dates, etc. NOT the tutor's. If the tutor is present in the class, then it may be handled differently with the tutor explaining the assignment. However, the tutor is not the professor and the tutee should not ask or expect the tutor to repeat a missed lecture.

2. Tutees must read class material, texts, handouts, supplementary material, etc., before attending class and before attending the tutoring session. The tutees should be encouraged to review their class notes daily.

3. Tutees should come to the tutoring session prepared. After the first introductory session, there should be no reason for the tutee to come to a session without being ready to work and this should be very succinctly explained during the first session.

4. Tutees should come to the tutoring session willing to be active participants. This is what often differentiates the tutoring session from the class setting. There is the opportunity in the tutoring session for real give-and-take participation that is not always present in the class.

Methods and techniques

Tutoring is a challenging experience, and effective tutors will have at their disposal a variety of methods and techniques. Tutors will want to adapt and modify any method or technique to meet the individual needs of their tutees. Some techniques will be fairly straightforward, others involve a more circuitous approach, but whatever the approach, flexibility will be the cornerstone. Flexibility means that the tutor realizes that not all methods or techniques will be successful with all tutees and tries something else. Flexibility also means that the tutor realizes that some techniques or methods may not be appropriate to use with certain tutees and always takes into account the personal and cultural differences, comfort levels, and preferred learning styles, etc. when engaging the tutee(s).

When working with the tutee who needs minimal content area help, one of the most straightforward methods is simply letting the tutee start work. The tutor goes over the assignment with the tutee, ascertains that the tutee understands the directions and the requirements of the assignment and then lets the tutee begin work. The tutor must "check in" periodically with the tutee (i.e., every 15 minutes or so), to ensure that the tutee is still on target and asks if there are any questions or concerns, addresses those, and then goes on. This method lets the tutee have an anchor with the tutor while exploring the assignment on his/her own.

Some tutees will need more specific help. The tutor could, after diagnosing the areas of concern with the tutee, suggest a specific step-by-step approach. By delineating the process with the tutee, the tutor then leaves the tutee to work on point one. Example: when the tutee is working in a workbook the tutor would review the directions with the tutee; stand by while the tutee works through a few examples; check those examples and discuss them with the tutee; provide more examples; and let the tutee work on those examples for a specific period of time. Checking at the end of the allotted and agreed-upon time and reviewing with the tutee the work completed, the tutee will probably be ready to move to step two and so on.

Some may recognize this as a variation on successive approximation from general psychology class. Yes, it is, and it is an effective technique. By letting the tutee progress at his/her own rate through a process with success at each step as the reward, the goal of the desired end behavior can be reached without undue stress for the tutee or tutor.

It is not always possible, however, to give unlimited time to the acquisition of an end behavior or skill. A variation would be to piggy back skills and to address two or three skills at a time. Again, this can be done with a workbook in the tutoring session and supplemented with extra examples to be done by the tutee before the next session. At the next session, the homework is reviewed and discussed, and may be reinforced by asking the tutee to self-check with several more examples; and then move on. Any of these methods can easily be done one on one or while working with several tutees with similar difficulties.

Another method/technique that can be successful is a variation of role-reversal. This is like the old adage: you don't really know something until you have to teach it to someone else. After the tutee has gained mastery of a particular skill or has overcome a particular area of difficulty, the tutor asks the tutee to "teach or tutor it back." This can give the tutee another way of looking at the skill and help instill a sense of confidence with the skill.

Yet another variation might be to ask the tutee what she/he thinks the first step might be in mastering a skill, the second step, third and so on. This can give the tutee a real sense that there is a process, as well as a scope and sequence to the skill while at the same time enhancing the tutee's critical thinking skills.

Other methods and techniques include game reviews which can be done one on one or in a group situation. A variation on *Jeopardy!* with a group of tutees can be a fun and very worthwhile review or exit activity. The tutees can actively participate by providing the "answers" to the categories (skill areas) the tutor provides. The tutees can then draw at random the "answers" and provide the appropriate question and an example.

Example 1:
    Category: Parts of Speech
    Answer: ". . . tells what the subject is doing and when the subject does the action."
    Question: "What is an action verb?"
    Example: "Mac correctly answered the question."

Example 2:
    Category: Punctuation
    Answer: ". . . joins two independent clauses whose ideas and sentence structure are related."
    Question: "What is one use for a semicolon?"
    Example: "Kacee wanted to go to the movies; Phoebe Anne phoned the theatre for the show times."

Whatever the methods or techniques the tutor uses, it is crucial for the tutor to have an understanding of individual learning styles. Is the tutee an auditory learner, a visual learner, or a hands-on learner? If the tutee is an auditory learner, the tutor may enhance the tutoring session by making audio tapes for the tutee. These tapes may have examples, directions, self-tests, reviews, etc. for the tutee to listen to, complete, and then discuss with the tutor as the session ending activity. The tutee could also make her/his own audio study or review tapes to enhance the class or tutoring activities. A tutee may benefit from talking through a writing assignment on tape, making a verbal/auditory outline or brainstorming session, then progressing to the writing stage.

If the tutee is a visual learner, it may be beneficial for the tutor to introduce the concept or idea of mapping to complement traditional outlining. Many tutees benefit from being able to draw a picture or diagram of an assignment before putting it into words. A simple example of this for writing an essay discussing three causes of the American Civil War might be: Step one: draw a train. On the engine put the topic, on the first train car indicate what is going to be discussed first, i.e., the first cause, on the second car the second cause, on the third car the third cause. Step two: go back and load each car with details that will support, explain, or identify. Step three: look at the couplings of the cars, how the cars are joined to one another. In other words, what is the transition from one car (paragraph) to the other? Step four: add on the caboose or the summary. A concept map does not have to be a work of art; it only has to be a useful tool to help get thoughts on paper so they can be seen and then written about.

If the tutee is a hands-on learner, a variation of the concept of mapping may be useful. Instead of drawing a picture, the tutee could use index cards or sheets of paper to write ideas on and then rearrange them. A hands-on learner may benefit from working on a particular area of interest in the tutoring session and then transferring that process to the class topic. For example, if a tutee is experiencing difficulty writing a paper on an assigned topic, it may be helpful to start with something the tutee enjoys, like a hobby. If the tutee can discuss the step-by-step process of something he/she enjoys, it is sometimes easier to translate that to something else.

When working with special needs tutees, the tutor must be aware of a variety of things that can have special bearing on the techniques and methods used. There are many types of special needs ranging from sight and hearing impaired to the older, nontraditional student, to the underprepared student. When working with sight-impaired students, for example, tutors could provide audio-taped exercises, activities, explanations and examples or enlarged print materials. The tutor must remember that detailed descriptions and specificity are crucial for the sight-impaired student; and the tutor realizes that more time may be needed to address skill areas and allows for this in the tutoring sessions.

When working with hearing-impaired tutees, the tutor will want to become aware of the proper procedure to use when working with the tutee and his/her signer. The tutor must be cognizant of the fact that he/she is working with and speaking with the tutee and to direct questions, answers, comments, and discussions to the tutee and not the signer. The tutor will want to use more visuals, diagrams, handouts, etc. and the tutor will provide a copy for the signer as well. The tutor should be aware of where she/he is sitting or standing in relation to the tutee—it is best to be across from rather than beside the tutee with the signer close beside the tutor.

Tutors are also advised that American Sign Language is a language, not just a system of signals, so some concepts do not translate easily. When a tutee is having difficulty it is crucial to have several variations, explanations or examples readily at hand to share with the tutee. Hearing-impaired tutees may read lips, so tutors should always be aware of possible "word filters" that can interfere: their head positions, back lighting, beards and mustaches, speaking very quickly, hands around the mouth, etc.

Mobility-impaired tutees may be working with a note-taker or writer so the tutor would want to take that into consideration when working with the tutee. Some tutees may require lap boards or special desks/tables in order to work most effectively.

The older or nontraditional tutee may need extra time to practice or at least dust off a skill that has not been used in a while, such as formal, academic writing or typing. The tutee may need time and encouragement to practice a newly acquired skill, such as using the computer.

Cultural differences are also factors to consider when tutoring. What may be perfectly acceptable in the tutor's culture may be just the opposite to the tutee—so when in doubt ask the tutee. "Shall I sit next to you or do you prefer that I sit across the table from you?" "You seem uncomfortable when I stand next to you while you are sitting and working. Is this inappropriate?" "Would you prefer to work with a female tutor (a male tutor)?" These may be appropriate questions to ask of any tutee when the tutor is in doubt.

Where can the tutor go for more information or additional resources concerning tutoring methods and techniques? Certainly the tutor should be aware of the help and support a professor can give. The writing professor may have instructor manuals, video or audio tapes, workbooks, exams, sample projects and assignments, a variety of textbooks, overhead transparencies, etc. that the tutor could use as tutoring adjuncts. A study skills professor may have similar material from his/her class that could be used to help address a particular deficit such as note taking or time management. A professor from another discipline may serve as a mentor to the tutor and offer particular insight about preparing written assignments for his/her particular discipline that the tutor could in turn share with tutees.

A very beneficial resource is other tutors. It is an extremely good idea for tutors to meet as a group to discuss and share ideas, concerns, problems, and successes. These meetings could be weekly or at least monthly. The tutor meetings could revolve around a specific topic or concern, for example: "How to tutor the reluctant tutee." This could provide tutors with a forum to share what has worked or what has not worked for them. The meetings could involve specific tutoring techniques such as role playing. Veteran tutors could assume the role of a reluctant tutee and novice tutors would take on the regular tutor role. By rehearsing in a role-playing situation, the novice tutors are given a chance to "try on" techniques and get immediate feedback from the veterans. Tutors can offer one another support, solace, advice, and reinforcement.

The tutor meetings could also include a guest speaker or discussion leader. The guest speaker could be a content area professor, a counselor, a coach, the tutor supervisor/trainer, a tutor from a different tutoring center or department on campus, a community leader, a member of the minority students affairs office or disabled student services, or one of the cultural organizations or clubs from campus.

Whatever the methods and techniques used, and the adaptations and variations made to them, the goal of tutoring is to help the tutee become a self-sufficient and successful student.

Recruitment

Where are the tutors to be found? Well, the answer may be surprising.

Perhaps the first place to start is right within the class. There are usually very skillful students in all classes who would be very good subject area tutors. They may be hesitant to come forward on their own, but the professor would certainly have an idea of who in the class might be an appropriate candidate after the first four or six weeks of the semester. If there are several sessions of the same class, the professor may want to recruit tutors from class A to tutor students in class B and vise versa. Former students are also good candidates to contact.

Professors may try recruiting from other classes in the department. Upper level writing students or graduate students might be the perfect candidates to tutor in the developmental or first-year writing classes. Students who are majors in disciplines other than English but who are English minors may be good prospects as are students majoring in disciplines that require good writing, for example, history or philosophy.

Schools or colleges of education may also be prime places to solicit tutors. Elementary or secondary education majors may welcome the opportunity to practice and hone skills, perhaps as part of a practicum course.

Existing tutoring centers on campus may have a surplus of tutors or underused tutors already trained and ready to go.

It is not uncommon to find retirees either on campus or in the community with specific skills who are more than willing to take on the role of tutor. A retired elementary or secondary school teacher, a retired English or writing professor, a former journalist, or professional writer may be a real boon to the tutoring community.

Specific student agencies on campus such as disabled student services or advising and counseling may be a source for tutors who already have specific tutor training in working with special needs students.

Cultural organizations or clubs on campus or in the community may be the place to seek tutors who have bilingual skills that would be beneficial.

Sororities, fraternities, or service organizations on campus may provide tutors as part of the group's community service commitment.

Athletic departments, departmental clubs, or organizations are also places to investigate.

Announcements may be aired on the college or university radio and/or TV station; as well as articles placed in the school and community newspapers. Additionally, notices can be placed on bulletin boards in the writing lab, classrooms, department offices, student center, counseling center, etc.

The next question is: "What about compensation?" Most tutors are volunteers but there are ways of expressing appreciation for their hard work when monetary compensation is not an option.

—Extra credit or independent study credit if tutors come from the class or from other classes in the department.

—Tuition waiver for the course: this, of course, would be dependent upon department or school policy.

—Textbook allowance for a course.

—Certifications of appreciation presented during the school's annual awards ceremony.

—Special recognition certificates or awards from the dean's office, department chair, and/or writing lab director.

—Inscribed plaque with tutors' names displayed in the department or writing lab.

—Articles in the school and community newspapers describing the tutors' contributions and a listing of their names.

—Announcements of appreciation on campus radio or TV and/or community stations.

—The opportunity to register early for certain department classes that tend to close or fill early.

—An end-of-the-semester party, luncheon, or dinner for tutors sponsored by the department or writing lab.

—A detailed letter of appreciation from the professor, department chair, and/or writing lab supervisor that the tutor can use as a reference letter or in a résumé or vita.

—Other possibilities include: special T-shirts, coffee mugs, tote bags, hats, discount arrangement with the bookstore or campus center, etc.

As with any job that is important but not recompensed, it is crucial for the workers, in this case, the tutors, to know that what they do is important, respected and appreciated.

Tutor training

The people who become tutors have content area expertise, skill, or knowledge and a desire to share that expertise, skill, or knowledge; otherwise, why would they want to be tutors? What these tutors may be lacking are some specific "tutoring skills." Certainly these skills can be picked up by trial and error, but this may hinder and interfere with the tutoring process. **It is especially important to train tutors in some specific tutoring skills before they actually start working with the tutees.** Creating a packet of material for tutors is also helpful and allows tutors to revisit procedures and to look up answers they may have as they tutor.

What should tutor training include? The following is a list of topics and suggestions that the professors, writing lab personnel and novice tutors can adapt and modify according to the specific needs of the students served.

Tutors can be trained in the following tutoring skill areas:

1. Definition of tutoring and specific tutor and tutee responsibilities as defined by the department or lab. This includes tutoring ethics and the tutoring philosophy of the particular program or department.
2. Basic tutoring guidelines, i.e., where tutoring will be done, when it will be done, by whom, to what end, what will and will not be included, etc.
3. How to successfully begin and end a tutoring session (one-on-one and group sessions).
4. Tutoring "do's" and "don'ts."
5. Role modeling general student success strategies and behaviors. This includes modeling specific problem-solving techniques.
6. Appropriate goal-setting and planning strategies.
7. Effective communication skills; how to appropriately question the tutee; how to effectively lead a discussion or begin a discussion.
8. Active, effective listening skills; paraphrasing.
9. How to refer the student to another resource, agency, etc. and when it is appropriate to do so.
10. Critical thinking skills and how to incorporate them into the tutoring session.
11. Specific study skills to share with the tutees: textbook-reading strategies such as the SQ3R, Cornell note-taking system or other ways to take more effective class notes, test-taking techniques, concentration, memory improvement techniques, time management, outlining, stress management, basic library skills, vocabulary development, etc.
12. Characteristics of adult learners and different learning styles.
13. Cultural awareness and sensitivity as well as cross-cultural communications; gender and age difference awareness; awareness of special needs/abilities.
14. Diagnostic techniques.
15. Recordkeeping.
16. Group management skills; group dynamics and group interactions.
17. Assertiveness training.
18. How to deal effectively with problem situations.
19. How to structure the tutoring experience.
20. How to use different tutoring approaches and tools more effectively, for example: how to make and use overhead transparencies, how and when to use computer programs, how to make and use audio or video tapes, supplementary resources, etc.

21. How to use positive reinforcement and praise to instill a sense of accomplishment in the tutee.

22. How to train other tutors; supervisory and management skills.

This list may be expanded or shortened according to the needs of the particular class or writing lab, but it is important that the tutors have a minimum level of training before they actually begin tutoring. It is important for the tutors and others involved to realize that there is more to successful tutoring than content area expertise and a desire to share that expertise. Help with the tutor training may be readily available on campus from former tutors, study skills professors, other tutoring centers on campus, learning and resource centers, or advising and counseling centers.

Students enter schools and are introduced to many different types of academic tools: resource books, computer programs, maps, charts, diagrams, equations, definitions, and theories. It is important to also introduce the student to another very important and helpful academic tool: the tutor.

For more information:

Gier, Tom, and Karan Hancock, eds. *Tutor Training Handbook*. Anchorage, Alaska: College Reading & Learning Association, 1996.

MacDonald, Ross B. *The Master Tutor: A Guidebook for more Effective Tutoring*. Williamsville, NY: The Cambridge Stratford Study Skills Institute, 1994.

Maxwell, Martha, ed. *From Access to Success: A Book of Readings on College Developmental Education and Learning Assistance Programs*. Clearwater, FL: H & H Publishing Company, Inc., 1994.

Maxwell, Martha, ed. *When Tutor Meets Student*. 2nd ed. Ann Arbor: The University of Michigan Press, 1994.

Myers, Lynda B. *Becoming an Effective Tutor*. Los Altos, CA: Crisp Publications, Inc. 1990.

APPENDIX A

CLASSROOM HANDOUTS

THE ELEMENTS OF GOOD WRITING

Writers should pay attention to five important basic areas if they are going to communicate well:

Coherence
Audience
Prewriting
Unity
Purpose

(Think CAP UP, or of someone flipping the brim of his or her baseball cap up before getting down to business!)

Prewriting is an important stage to any writing project. Prewriting helps a writer discover what he or she knows and thinks about the topic of a given writing project. Clustering, freewriting, listing, outlining, blind writing (writing on the computer with the monitor off), and doodling are all great methods of prewriting. Remember, the goal of prewriting is to "find yourself in the topic" and generate a number of ideas and images very quickly.

"Audience" is from the same root word as "audio" (audire, to hear) and means literally "people who hear." Who needs to hear the message you are writing about? Who would benefit the most? An audience for a piece of writing could be your family (a note on the refrigerator), your best friend (a letter), your boss (a memo or e-mail), or you may wish to reach a group of people—older students who work, third graders, people your age, people who ride motorcycles. The list is endless. The point is, you define whom you want to reach (whom you want to hear you). Then tailor your language and approach accordingly.

Purpose. Why are you writing the piece? Many times a writer cannot answer that question until halfway through a draft or even after. Your purpose may be to inform your audience. You may wish to entertain them. Do you have a point to prove? Are you going to tell a story, make a comparison, give examples, show how to do something, or describe something in detail? Know, before the final draft, what you wish to accomplish. The best finished writing contains forethought. Think ahead.

Unity. Any piece of writing you do should be a unified whole. That means you should have a clear thesis. Each paragraph should have either a topic sentence or main idea. Your paragraphs should clearly relate back to the thesis.

Coherence. Coherence is often confused with Unity, but here is the difference: Coherence is about the relationship of the sentences to one another. In order for your ideas to flow, it is important that you use transitional words and phrases. You want to make sure that one thought follows logically and clearly from another. Also, you will want to check that your sentences are organized according to an understandable scheme (most important to least important, least important to most important, chronologically, spatially, etc.).

Harcourt, Inc.

FINDING SUBJECTS AND VERBS 1

One of the most important things you must be able to do in a millisecond if you are going to be able to punctuate correctly is locate the subject(s) and verb(s) of any clause.

Subjects usually answer to the question, "Who or what is the sentence about? Who or what is performing the action?"

Subjects are often nouns or pronouns (a word that takes the place of a noun: *I, you, he, she, it, we, they*).

The subject can be a compound: two or more nouns or pronouns can be joined together by *and, or, either/or, neither/ nor.*

Since the **subject and verb of a sentence can never be found in a prepositional phrase,** delete all prepositional phrases from your sentence and see what's left.

> **By the back door, down in a drainage ditch,**
> **in the standing water, Sally caught seven**
> **tadpoles in a mayonnaise jar.**

> **Sally caught seven tadpoles.**

The subject and verb of a sentence will never be found in an appositive, a word or phrase that renames a subject or object. Therefore, identifying and deleting appositives is a good idea.

> **My brother John is a psychiatrist.**

> **My brother is a psychiatrist.**

FINDING SUBJECTS AND VERBS 2

If a sentence that is not a question begins with a verb and gives a command, the subject of the sentence is an **understood "you."**

Close that window.

(You) close that window.

The words *here* and *there* can never be the subject of a sentence, so look elsewhere for the subject (usually following a linking verb).

Here is the pencil.

There are no more apples.

Linking verbs can be the only verb in a sentence. They often look like helping verbs: is, are, was, were, am, have been, seem, become, remain, taste, look, smell, feel, sound.

Richard is tired.

A verb is not complete unless it contains all of the necessary helping verbs or modal auxiliaries that form an English verb tense.

By next summer, I will have been trying to
complete my master's degree for four years.

EXERCISE IN CONNOTATION

I. The following groups of words have the same *denotation* or basic definition; choose which of the choices has a negative sound or *connotation* and which has a positive connotation? Can you identify the reasons for your choices? Do any words in each group have a neutral connotation?

  When you have made your choices, find a partner to compare choices. It is possible that you will not agree in every case. Think about why this might be the case. Is it possible that you are both right, depending on the context?

  1. procrastinate/hesitate/stall/play for time/hold off/delay
  2. weak/flabby/feeble/soft/gutless/weakly/sluggish/dull/bloodless
  3. energetic/vigorous/forceful/powerful/intense/dynamic/strong/demonic
  4. stench/stink/smell/odor/fetidness/noxiousness/miasma/reek/rankness
  5. quiet/silent/deathlike/tomblike/still/noiseless/hush/tranquil
  6. intelligent/understanding/egg-headed/pin-headed/scholarly/witty/high IQ
  7. crazy/insane/madman or -woman/sick/ill/demented/deranged/lunatic
  8. dumb/simple/stupid/idiotic/ignorant/empty-headed/vacuous/unknowing
  9. trusting/unsuspicious/blind/credulous/uncritical/believing/gullible
  10. coarse/unrefined/clumsy/crude/natural/refreshing/down-to-earth
  11. impulsive/loose cannon/capricious/fun loving/fanciful/flighty
  12. ordinary/average/normal/commonplace/garden variety/unexceptional

II. For the following words, write several synonyms that have a more positive connotation and several which have a negative connotation. You may use words or phrases. For more ideas, check your thesaurus.

  1. clean
  2. tired
  3. untrustworthy
  4. expensive
  5. impatient
  6. marriage
  7. intoxicated
  8. illegal
  9. punishment
  10. anger
  11. acquire
  12. workplace
  13. excess
  14. prosperous

Harcourt, Inc.

EXERCISE IN
SOUND-ALIKES

It is easy to make mistakes with the following pairs of sound-alike words. Choose 10 pairs, and write a sentence for each pair in which the sound-alikes are used and spelled correctly. Look any new vocabulary up in your dictionary.

Example: In **addition** to receiving the Sunday paper, we are now getting the daily **edition.**

addition/edition
affect/effect
air/err/heir
aloud/allowed
amend/emend
aisle/isle
ant/aunt
assent/ascent
aural/oral
bear/bare
bazaar/bizarre
be/bee
berry/bury
blew/blue
boar/bore
bridal/bridle
bough/bow
but/butt
buy/by/bye
capital/capitol
carat/carrot/caret
cellar/seller
censer/censor
cents/sense
chute/shoot
coarse/course
complement/compliment
counsel/council
cowered/coward
currant/current
cymbal/symbol
dam/damn
die/dye
dear/deer
dew/due/do
descent/dissent
doe/dough
dual/duel
emit/omit
ensure/insure
I/eye
fairy/ferry

flour/flower
forward/foreword
gorilla/guerrilla
great/grate
groan/grown
hair/hare
hall/haul
halve/have
hear/here
him/hymn
heard/herd
hole/whole
hour/our
idol/idle
in/inn
intense/intents
its/it's
knead/need
knew/new
know/no
knot/not
lessen/lesson
liable/libel
lightening/lightning
loan/lone
mall/maul
manner/manor
metal/medal
made/maid
mail/male
meat/meet
mince/mints
morning/mourning
naval/navel
pair/pare/pear
pail/pale
palate/palette
parish/perish
past/passed
patience/patients
peace/piece
pedal/peddle

plait/plate
plum/plumb
pray/prey
presents/presence
principle/principal
rain/reign
raze/raise
read/red
real/reel
read/reed
residence/residents
ring/wring
rode/road
role/roll
sail/sale
saver/savor
sea/see
scene/seen
scent/sent
sects/sex
sight/site/cite
shone/shown
soul/sole
some/sum
son/sun
stairs/stares
steal/steel
taught/taut
tear/tier
than/then
throne/thrown
their/there/they're
to/too/two
tea/tee
thyme/time
toad/towed/told
waist/waste
weather/whether
whose/who's
would/wood
week/weak
write/right

Harcourt, Inc.

EXERCISE IN
NARRATION 1

Dialogue

The following exchange between two brothers has been written without fragments, dialect, and interruptions. First assignment: Write out the same dialogue the way that you, or someone you know, would speak. Second assignment: Rewrite the dialogue in a dialect of your choice. Third assignment: Write six sentences of your revised dialogue in direct quotation format, paying attention to placement of commas, quotes, and other marks of punctuation. For fun, look at Sam Shepard's dialogue choices in the opening scene of *True West*.

Speaker 1:   I heard that Mother decided to go to Alaska. Was that true?

Speaker 2:   Yes, it is true.

Speaker 1:   Did she leave you in charge of the house?

Speaker 2:   Yes, she did. She knew I was coming down to visit, so she offered to let me stay here.

Speaker 1:   Have you been watering all of the plants?

Speaker 2:   Yes, I have.

Speaker 1:   Have you been keeping the kitchen sink clean? You know that Mother does not like it if there is even a single tea leaf in the sink.

Speaker 2:   Yes, I know.

Speaker 1:   Will she be in Alaska for a long time?

Speaker 2:   I am not sure.

Speaker 1:   It must be nice for you to have the whole house to yourself.

Speaker 2:   Yes, I am enjoying it.

Speaker 1:   There are a lot of crickets around here. There are lots and lots of crickets. Do you have any food? Do you have any coffee?

Speaker 2:   What was that you said?

Speaker 1:   Do you have any coffee?

Speaker 2:   Yes, I do have coffee?

Speaker 1:   That is good. Is it real coffee and not instant coffee?

Speaker 2:   Yes, it is. Would you like some coffee?

Speaker 1:   No, thank you. I brought something of my own to drink.

Speaker 2:   Please help yourself to anything in the refrigerator.

Speaker 1:   Thank you, I will. Please do not worry about me. I can take care of myself.

EXERCISE IN
NARRATION 2

In the following story, events are told out of chronological sequence. Create a chronological outline of the events described. Rewrite the selection according to your outline, supplying details as necessary.

My step-father and step-brother were on vacation in Washington when I decided to leave home. I knew that if I was ever going to leave home, it had to be then. My step-father was a very stern man who had strong views on what an American family should be. However, he wasn't acting like much of a father to me. He was only concerned with maintaining a close relationship with his son. He always sided with Robert, my step-brother, regardless of the situation. Therefore, I typically got in trouble for things I didn't even do. I promptly did my chores every day after school while Josh, my step-brother, sat on his lazy butt and watched television. It shocked my step-father when I left. He never really realized how much I did around the house, nor did he realize how much of a jerk he had been until after I left and it was too late. Just last year he formally apologized for being so cruel all of those years. It must be very difficult for a man with that much pride to apologize to a young man like myself. I admire that very much. I forgave him completely, and since then we have become very close friends.

The stress I endured around the house was unbelievable. This is what eventually drove me to leave. I was only a twelve-year-old boy living a life of "torture." One time, I remember sitting at the table for two hours because I wouldn't eat my entire bowl of soup. My step-father had a strict policy of "take all you want, but eat all you take!" Mom had made some vegetable-beef soup with chunks of meat in it. The meat was very hard; it was too tough for my jaws to handle. If I could have just swallowed the meat, then I could have left the table, but the meat was just too large to swallow and it was just too tough for my tired jaws to shred. I refused to eat it. I sat there for two hours staring at the meat until finally he let me leave. This was one of the few occasions that I won the battle. Constant fighting amongst parents over money, super-strict rules set by my step-father, and constant hatred between my step-brother and me eventually led to my leaving.

From "My Train Of Life" by Gary Myrick

EXERCISE IN DESCRIPTION

In the following paragraph, add specific details (concrete nouns, adjectives, adverbs, active verbs) to make the writing more vivid.

When I was young, I lived with my family in a small house in a Western state. At that time, things were not going well. My mother had remarried and her new husband had brought his child to live with us. Home life was a constant challenge and difficult to come to terms with. I decided it was time for a change. The decision I made changed the lives of my family members as well as my own.

In the following example, underline the descriptions which seem the most vivid to you. Try to write a descriptive paragraph about your class partner.

Throughout Anita's interview, her blonde hair stayed tucked behind her ears. Her green, Barbara Streisand eyes were concentrated on her nails as she bit them the same way a mouse nibbles on cheese. Her slender figure sat Indian style on my floor as she blurted out stories of her middle school, high school, and college experiences.

In the following example, change ten words and/or phrases to give the scene a sense of foreboding.

It was an unusually hot morning. As we pulled into the dusty parking lot that had only about ten or eleven other cars in it, I gazed to my left, then to my right. To my left I saw a trailer and two enormous planes. To my right nothing but open field and sky. As we filed out of the temperature-controlled van into the blistering sun, I was beginning to wonder what I had gotten myself into.

EXERCISE IN
SUPPORTING DETAILS

Give four examples for each topic sentence to explain, illustrate or clarify the idea.

Topic Sentence: Last winter was the worst winter I have ever experienced.

1.

2.

3.

4.

Topic Sentence: Choosing to remodel the house myself was a huge mistake.

1.

2.

3.

4.

Topic Sentence: Camping can be physically, emotionally, and spiritually exhausting.

1.

2.

3.

4.

Create two thesis statements of your own and list four supporting examples for each.

Harcourt, Inc.

TWO COMPARISON OR CONTRAST
ESSAY OUTLINES

Block Outline

I. Introduction: Introduce both of your subjects that you will be comparing or contrasting. You may do this by telling a story which mentions both, telling two brief contrasting anecdotes, or giving background information about both (just to name a few possibilities).

II. Body.

    A. Subject 1.

        1. Attribute 1.

        2. Attribute 2.

        3. Attribute 3.

    B. Subject 2.

        1. Attribute 1.

        2. Attribute 2.

        3. Attribute 3.

III. Conclusion: You might explain the meaning of the comparison or contrast of your subjects, tell your reader why Subject 2 is superior/inferior to Subject 1 based on the information you provide (or vice versa), among other things.

Point-by-Point Outline

I. Introduction: Introduce Subjects 1 and 2 (same as above).

II. Body.

    A. Attribute 1.

        1. Subject 1.

        2. Subject 2.

    B. Attribute 2.

        1. Subject 1.

        2. Subject 2.

    C. Attribute 3.

        1. Subject 1.

        2. Subject 2.

III. Conclusion: (Same as above.)

Note: You may have more than three attributes for comparison or contrast. You may not have more than two subjects.

PRACTICE IN COMPARISON OR CONTRAST

Organize the following supporting details into 1.) a block outline, and 2.) a point-by-point outline:

Laundry 1898 and 1998

1. My grandmother boiled water for laundry in the same black cauldron where she made lye soap.
2. She shaved a bar of lye soap into chips which she put in the boiling water.
3. After sorting her family's clothes, she placed several items of clothing into the soapy water and boiled them for a few minutes.
4. She lifted each piece of clothing out of the water with a sturdy hardwood stick.
5. She rubbed any stain with a bar of lye soap.
6. She scrubbed the clothes on a ripply washboard.
7. She rinsed clothes in another tub of cold water.
8. She wrung out the clothes in a ringer.
9. Afterwards, she took the clothes outside and pinned them to the clothesline.
10. Then she ironed everything.
11. She heated the flat irons on her wood cookstove.
12. At last, she would fold each item of clothing or hang it in the oak wardrobe.

1. I buy my soap, which comes in powdered or liquid form, at the grocery store.
2. I also buy bleach, stain remover, and fabric softener (either liquid or sheets).
3. I sort my clothes and use stain remover on any spots I find.
4. I set my automatic washing machine to the proper setting and put soap in the machine as it fills.
5. I place the clothes, sorted according to color and fabric, in the machine.
6. The hot water comes from a gas water heater through the pipes into the machine.
7. After the cycle is finished, about twenty minutes later, I take the clothes out of the washing machine.
8. I quickly place them in the automatic dryer, along with a fabric softening sheet.
9. I choose the correct setting by turning a knob.
10. Then I press a button to start the dryer.
11. When the clothes are dry, I take them out and only need to iron a few items with an electric iron.
12. Finally, I fold the clothes and put them in a chest of drawers or hang them in the closet.

BASIC CLASSIFICATION AND DIVISION OUTLINE

I. Introduction: Introduce the subject you wish to classify and give your overall classes. Make it interesting.

II. Body: Give all classes in a logical fashion and follow with good examples of each class.

    A. Class 1.

        1. Example 1.

        2. Example 2.

        3. Example 3.

    B. Class 2.

        1. Example 1.

        2. Example 2.

        3. Example 3.

    C. Class 3.

        1. Example 1.

        2. Example 2.

        3. Example 3.

III. Conclusion: Explain what we can learn from using your particular system of classification.

Harcourt, Inc.

CAUSE AND EFFECT
ANALYSIS 1

Conducting Surveys and Polls

Advice on Conducting Surveys and Polls: When composing questions for surveys or polls which will attempt to discover patterns of opinion or behavior in a cross-section of people, it is important to ensure that each question gives rise to a limited number of responses. The questioner must give enough range in the possible responses so that those being surveyed or polled do not feel that they are being "led" to respond in predetermined patterns. Remember: the goal of good surveys and polls is to uncover truths, not to find answers which reinforce at all costs your particular position on an issue.

I. Choose one of the following survey topics and compose 10–15 questions which will have limited responses. When you are satisfied with your questionnaire, conduct your survey by finding a good cross-section of people, reading each question in a professional manner, and jotting down their responses to each of your questions:

1. You are researching the negative effects of sugar (particularly candy) on adult behavior. You wish to know more about the average candy consumption of the population.

2. You want to discover the causes of the general boom in interest in recycling. Compose questions that will determine recycling habits and/or opinions on the matter.

3. You are writing a report on the causes of teenage drug addiction. Survey a wide number of people, especially teenagers. Hint: go to a mall.

4. You wish to conduct a poll on the effects of the current political system on people's lives. Make sure you ascertain whether or not informants are aware of the current system. Ask about their political leanings. Ask for specific signs of growth or decline.

Note: Once you have conducted your survey, tabulate your answers and draw tentative conclusions based on your findings.

CAUSE AND EFFECT
ANALYSIS 2

Conducting Interviews

Advice on Interviewing: The principles of composing interview questions are nearly the opposite of those for surveys and polls. In an interview, you will devote a significant amount of time to listening to one person or a limited number of people. Your questions should therefore be as open ended as possible in an effort to elicit longer answers from the person being interviewed. The tone and phrasing in which an answer is given will be of interest to you. If your subject does not respond at first, part of your job is to probe into reasons for reticence. Many times interviewers find that using a tape recorder makes an in-depth interview feel more like a conversation.

Make an appointment to interview someone concerning the effects of education. Set a time limit (e.g., 20–30 minutes). When the interview is finished, choose three interesting answers and write down the direct, *verbatim* quote following your question.

EXERCISE IN
WRITING A DEFINITION

Choose one of the following concepts which you are familiar with to be the topic of your definition essay or paragraph. Follow the steps below.

1. College Educated	11. Afterlife
2. Long-term Goals	12. Religious Conviction
3. Role Model	13. Animal Instinct
4. Fast Food	14. Creative Thinking
5. Figure of Speech	15. Business Sense
6. Horse Sense	16. Oppression
7. "Sleep on It"	17. Happy Medium
8. Reverse Psychology	18. Nepotism
9. Culture	19. Flirting
10. Internet	20. Strategy

1. Once you have chosen a concept, **brainstorm** (e.g., freewrite, cluster, list, etc.) for at least **one page** about everything you know about the concept. The brainstorm will be submitted with the essay.

2. On a separate sheet of paper, create **your own three-sentence definition** of your concept.

3. Look up the word or words that make up the name of your concept in the dictionary, and **write down the definition(s)** beneath the definition you created.

4. Beneath the definitions, note **comparisons and conflicts** between your own definition and the dictionary's.

5. On another sheet of paper, write down **four detailed examples** of the concept that you have either experienced, heard about, or read about.

Harcourt, Inc.

EXERCISE IN
WRITING PROCESSES

Write clear and simple steps to the following processes, keeping in mind a particular audience. Use complete sentences and transitional words and phrases.

1. Write official directions to tell office workers how to use the Xerox machine properly.

2. Explain to a 10-year-old how to write a letter to complain about the safety features on his or her new in-line skates.

3. Tell a close friend how to dress for an important job interview:

4. Show a five-year-old how to make a favorite sandwich:

Harcourt, Inc.

SAMPLE TOPICS FOR PERSUASIVE ESSAYS

Below you will find a list of "hot" or newsworthy topics and a short list of sample personal topics for persuasive essays. The questions that follow the topics are certainly not the only areas of debate. When you pick a topic for a persuasive essay, you must find a focus that will be narrow enough to guide your research and help you to pick the most appropriate sources, facts, and statistics for your paper. As always, try to find a topic that you have an interest in finding out more about.

Hot Topics

Adoption (infants, older children, interracial)

Affirmative Action (positive effects, negative effects)

Alcoholism (Is it a disease? In conjunction with pregnancy)

Animals and Physical Therapy (Do pets aid the physically challenged?)

Breastfeeding (Is breastfeeding or formula feeding best for infants?)

Caffeine (Is it good or bad for you?)

Child Abuse (When does discipline become child abuse? What should be done to reform child abusers?)

Child Witnesses (Should children be allowed to testify in court?)

Cigarette Ads (Should cigarette ads be banned from magazines?)

Cigarette Companies (Should cigarette companies have to pay damages to smokers who have developed lung disease?)

Day Care (Is day care or home care best for young children?)

Drinking Age (What is the most appropriate drinking age?)

Drug Addiction (What are the best ways to stop teen addiction? What is the best way to reform an addict?)

Elder Care (What is the best way to care for elderly family members? What is the best way to care for Alzheimer's patients?)

Endangered Species (Are endangered species laws too strict or too lax?)

Euthanasia (Should it be legal or remain illegal?)

Farm Subsidies (Should small farmers receive federal aid to help them compete with agribusinesses?)

Foreign Language Requirement (Should a foreign language be a requirement for all high schoolers? When should foreign language instruction begin? What are the most useful languages for Americans to learn?)

Genetic Testing (Are some forms of genetic testing invasive or harmful?)

Global Warming (What can be done about it?)

Gun Control (What types of weapons, if any, should be controlled? Is the waiting period long enough or too long?)

Head Start Programs (Does Head Start significantly increase an under-advantaged child's chances for academic success?)

Internet (Should the Internet be regulated?)

Political Ads (Should political ads be monitored, screened for truthfulness, or regulated?)

Privacy in the Workplace (Should employers have the right to employees' e-mail, voice mail, etc.?)

APPENDIX B

ESSAY EVALUATION HANDOUTS

EDITING AND PROOFREADING

Complete the following checklist for editing before turning in final drafts:

1. Have I read my work aloud to listen for problems?

2. Did I check every possible misspelling in a dictionary or with a spell checker?

3. Did I edit for run-on sentences?

4. Did I edit for fragments?

5. Did I check my use of verbs?

6. Did I check my use of comma splices?

7. Did I check my use of pronouns?

8. Have I checked any punctuation I'm unsure of?

9. Have I checked my use of capital letters?

Harcourt, Inc.

PEER EVALUATION FOR EXPLORATION DRAFT

Student Writer _____

Student Evaluator _____

Thesis:

- Where has the author placed the thesis? Underline it.

- Is the thesis sufficiently narrow and interesting? If not, make several suggestions for narrowing or expanding the thesis.

- Is there a possible thesis lurking elsewhere in the paper that may be what the writer might prefer to write about?

Examples:

- Count the number of specific examples that support the thesis (an example might be a number, a statistic, a brief story, a clear description, a well-explained quote, etc.)

- Do you feel there are enough examples and details to support the thesis and hold your interest? If not, help the writer to brainstorm for more examples.

- Are the examples sufficiently sharp? Does the author use names, dates, titles, places, colors, shapes, etc.? Mark vague or uninteresting examples with an asterisk (*) in the margin of the paper.

Overall Impression:

- What do you especially admire in this draft? Are there any aspects you would like to emulate in your own writing?

- What would you like to know more about?

- What would you like for the writer to tell you in the conclusion?

Additional Comments:

Harcourt, Inc.

PEER EVALUATION
FOR ROUGH DRAFT

Student Writer _____

Student Evaluator _____

1. What strategy does the author use to grab your interest? Could the introduction be more exciting? If so, make several suggestions for improvement.

2. Do you want to read the essay from beginning to end? If not, put an arrow at the point where you begin to lose interest.

3. Underline the paper's thesis. Draw a wavy line under the topic sentence of each paragraph. If you cannot detect a topic sentence in a given paragraph, jot down the controlling idea in the margin of the paper.

4. Number the paragraphs in the paper. According to what principle are they organized?

5. Are there long paragraphs that are really two or more paragraphs in disguise? If so, write down the numbers of the corresponding paragraphs.

6. Are there any short paragraphs that really belong with another paragraph? If so, give the numbers of the paragraphs.

7. How do you feel at the conclusion? Does the author sufficiently sum things up and leave you feeling satisfied? Are there loose ends that leave you hanging? Make several suggestions for improvement.

8. Copy one of the paragraphs of the paper into your journal and revise by deleting unnecessary words and phrases, adding specific examples, and reorganizing material for better rhetorical effect as necessary. When you are satisfied with what you have done, share the revision with the author with the understanding that your revision is one of many possible ways to revise and edit.

9. What do you admire about the author's style, use of language, storytelling ability, clarity, precision of details, musicality, etc.?

ROUGH DRAFT EVALUATION
OF ESSAY

Student: _____

Focus:

Does the paper have a narrowed thesis?

Do the paragraphs have topic sentences or controlling ideas that clearly relate to the thesis?

20 points possible.

Organization:

Do the ideas follow a logical progression?

Are there adequate transitional paragraphs, words, and phrases?

Does the writer use a clear pattern of organization in both body and paragraphs?

20 points possible.

Development:

Are there enough details, statistics, facts, and examples to make the writer's position clear and to define concepts?

Is there adequate explanation of quotations?

Are examples and quotations appropriate and well integrated?

20 points possible.

Introduction and Conclusion:

Does the introduction grab the reader's attention and show signs of technique and attention to audience?

Does the conclusion sufficiently wrap up loose ends and leave the reader with a provocative thought?

10 points possible for each.

Grammar and Mechanics:

More than 4 major usage errors, or 2 major usage errors and 4 additional errors, or 8 minor errors will result in a score of 0.

20 points possible.

Total points out of 100 =

Instructor's Comments and Suggestions for Revision:

GRAMMAR AND MECHANICS EVALUATION

Major Usage Errors

Fused run-ons   _____

"And" run-ons   _____

Comma splices   _____

Fragments   _____

Minor Comma Errors

Excessive comma use   _____

No comma after introductory phrase   _____

No comma after introductory clause   _____

No commas around nonrestrictive modifiers   _____

No commas around vocatives/sentence adverbs   _____

Spelling, Quotation, and Capitalization

Capitalization errors   _____

Spelling errors   _____

Sound-alike word misspellings   _____

Look-alike word misuse   _____

Quotation punctuation errors   _____

Agreement

Subject-verb agreement errors   _____

Pronoun-antecedent agreement errors   _____

Pronoun case errors   _____

Faulty parallelism   _____

Modifiers

Dangling modifiers   _____

Misplaced modifiers   _____

Verbs:

Wrong verb tense   _____

Sequence of tenses errors   _____

Unnecessary shifts in verb tense   _____

Style:

Inadequate use of subordination   _____

Inadequate use of coordination   _____

Inadequate use of transitions   _____

Overuse of the same sentence structure   _____

Overuse of vague/abstract terms   _____

FIRST REVISION EVALUATION
OF ESSAY

Student: _____

Focus:

20 points possible.

Organization:

10 points possible.

Development:

20 points possible.

Introduction and Conclusion:

20 points possible.

Grammar and Mechanics:

10 points possible.

Improvement:

20 points possible.

Total points out of 100 =

SECOND REVISION EVALUATION
OF ESSAY

Student: _____

Focus:

20 points possible.

Organization:

20 points possible.

Development:

25 points possible.

Introduction and Conclusion:

10 points possible.

Grammar and Mechanics:

5 points possible.

Improvement:

20 points possible.

Total points out of 100 =

Harcourt, Inc.

IN-CLASS ESSAY EVALUATION

Student clearly refers to article:	**5 points**
Examples are clearly rendered and appropriate:	**5 points**
Student quotes accurately and faithfully:	**5 points**
Thesis is clearly the product of rigorous thought:	**5 points**
Student addresses an academic audience:	**5 points**
Tone is consistent throughout:	**5 points**
Introduction demonstrates writing technique:	**5 points**
Student concludes essay in a final paragraph:	**5 points**
Conclusion is more than a mere summary of the body:	**5 points**
Student's work has been carefully proofread:	**5 points**
Student has employed a complex vocabulary:	**5 points**
Student has a good sense of language flow and phrasings:	**5 points**
Student has a clear thesis:	**10 points**
Student addresses essay question:	**10 points**
Paragraphs are coherent and advance thesis idea:	**10 points**
Student's work is virtually free of usage errors:	**10 points**

Subtotal:

Name, course number, or section number missing:	**minus 1 point**
Title missing or overly vague/general:	**minus 1 point**

Subtotal:

Minus deductions:

Total:

Harcourt, Inc.

GROUP WORK EVALUATION

Group successfully completed assignment (as much as was possible within the given time):	Y / N
Group strove to write complex thoughts and sentences:	Y / N
Group grasped the core idea behind assignment:	Y / N
All members of group participated in assignment:	Y / N

Comments:

SUMMARY EVALUATION

Student mentions author, title, and thesis:	Y / N
Student uses strong verbs:	Y / N
Student accurately represents author's position:	Y / N
Student notes all main points:	Y / N
Student adequately paraphrases/quotes:	Y / N
Student uses correct grammar:	Y / N
Student uses varied sentence structure:	Y / N

Comments:

PARAGRAPH EXAM
OVER COMPARISON/CONTRAST
AND CAUSE/EFFECT

Directions:

Choose two of the following topics and create a well-written, fully supported paragraph for each. You must choose one topic from the Comparison/Contrast category and one from the Cause/Effect category. It is your responsibility to narrow and define the topics into workable topic sentences (main ideas).

Your Comparison/Contrast paragraph must follow either the **block** or **point-by-point** structure with at least three points of comparison. Your Cause/Effect should be strictly cause (covering **immediate causes, remote causes, and influences**) *or* effect (covering **immediate effects and long-term effects**). Make sure that each of your paragraphs makes sense, is well organized, and has at least three **major details,** three corresponding **minor details,** appropriate **transitional words** and/or phrases, and a **concluding statement.**

Use the pages provided to do your prewriting (brainstorming/clustering/listing) to help you generate ideas for the paragraphs. Write your paragraphs on the lined paper provided (use the back of the sheets if necessary). Good luck!

Topics for Comparison/Contrast

1. Compare or contrast riding a bicycle to riding a motorcycle.

2. Compare or contrast watching movies to watching videos.

3. Compare or contrast two restaurants.

4. Compare or contrast two places you have lived.

5. Compare or contrast two jobs you have held or wish to hold.

Topics for Cause/Effect

1. The causes or the effects of excessive salaries for professional sports

2. The causes or the effects of the Internet on modern lifestyles

3. The causes or the effects of rapidly changing technology

4. The causes or the effects of watching too much television

5. The causes or the effects of eating a high cholesterol diet

FINAL EXAM ESSAY TOPICS

Directions: Choose one of the following topics and write a well-developed essay according to the ideas we have discussed in class. Make sure that your essay has a thesis, an introduction and a conclusion, topic sentences for the body paragraphs, and plenty of details. Spend at least ten minutes on prewriting and defining/narrowing your topic before you begin the initial draft. Good idea: Make a scratch outline of your paragraphs. Proofread your work very carefully. Your final draft should be 200–300 words long (about two and one-half, handwritten, double-spaced pages/one full page typed and double-spaced). You must turn in all drafts and notes with your essay, but put the final version (with its clever, appropriate title!) on top.

1. Describe a person you are close to in terms of appearance and/or personality and/or habits.

2. Describe, using good concrete details, a beautiful or a horrible place you have visited.

3. Tell a story about a funny and/or embarrassing event in your life (be sure to have a point to the story!).

4. Tell a story about a moment that changed you and/or the way you thought about a particular issue.

5. Compare or contrast two restaurants you have been to; then evaluate strengths and weaknesses.

6. Compare or contrast two television programs you have watched; then evaluate strengths and weaknesses.

7. Explain to an entering freshman the process of registering for classes, becoming a better student, preparing for a test, or surviving a six-week summer course.

8. Explain the process of making a particular food that you like (e.g., nachos, pizza, lemonade, etc.) for someone who does not know how to cook very well.

Harcourt, Inc.

APPENDIX C

SAMPLE STUDENT WRITINGS

STUDENT ILLUSTRATION

Worst Vacation

By Josie Heyman

I had the worst vacation at the beach. I was there with my family including four children. First, I lost my nephew. It was a crowded weekend with people everywhere. I looked up, and he was gone. I panicked and started asking everyone if he or she had seen him. After about ten minutes, I sent my husband to the life-guard stand and went to find his mother. I was relieved to find them together. As if that wasn't enough, I was going out for a swim when I felt an awful stinging in my legs. I rushed out of the water to find I had been stung by a Man 'o war jellyfish. He had apparently gotten tangled in my legs. I had been stung from the tops of my thighs to my ankles. To top that, I had an allergic reaction a week later. Finally, I went to the hotel room to soothe the stinging to find I had been out in the sun too long. I was sunburned from head to toe. I was never so ready for a vacation to be over.

STUDENT DESCRIPTION

Easter

By Daniel Wolbert

It is early afternoon on a beautiful sunny Easter Sunday just warm enough to wear shorts and short-sleeved shirts. The remnants of fall leaves still pepper the ground. The grass is starting to poke green blades up in some spots, but it is still brown in others. The shade from the naked tree limbs cast intriguing shadows on the ground. You can still see the hillside through the limbs. The cedar trees are at their brightest green of the year, before the insects and heat of summer has turned them brown.

A small dog in the distance watches intently as a father and son hunt Easter eggs hidden earlier by the boy's mother, just enough easy ones to keep his interest and some hidden deep in leaves and holes to make it last. The boy follows his father hoping he will spot the more elusive eggs he missed. The boy is filled with excitement about the magic of the day, peering intently at the ground, hoping to spot andother brightly colored egg.

The boy carries a yellow basket that is almost as big as he is, holding it with both hands, trying to keep the treasure within from falling out and breaking on the ground.

I was a simple moment in time that will last for a lifetime in the memories of a father and his son.

STUDENT NARRATIVE

Festus

By Malona Zolliecoffer

Our friends were not home the hot summer day I went to pick him out. As I made my way up to the pen where he was, many puppies come out of a make-shift dog house. They all wiggled, jumped, and licked me through the ratty chicken wire, hoping to be the chosen one. He met my eye quickly. He was light tan and white and had wrinkles from head to toe. Little did I know the future he held with me would leave me in wonder and despair. I named him Festus.

His first year with me brought me lots of laughs, joy, and play. But I will never forget that sultry summer afternoon. He lay motionless against a white lawn chair. He drew my attention by bounding to the back side of the house. Terror went over me as I thought of the worst that could happen—Parvo? We spent many dollars, many vet trips and sleepless nights to bring him back to the dog I once had known.

The following summer came soon, and many memories of him became stamped in my mind. Photos, outside play, and rides on the four-wheeler revolved around him.

Saturday afternoon we left the house. Festus and Ivory stood on the hill in front of our country home. They often went there to play and watch the neighbor's cattle.

On Sunday we spent the day walking and riding four-wheelers, looking for a clue, a trail, or a corpse. He had vanished without a trace as though God had decided it was his time to go. That day still haunts me in my heart, and tears still cloud my eyes at the thought of him. It is a mystery unsolved over a dog named Festus. He will be in my heart forever. I still love him.

STUDENT COMPARISON/CONTRAST

Water Pipes: Copper or P.V.C.?
By Daniel Wolbert

Choosing water piping for your new or existing home can be a difficult and even costly decision. Most professionals think copper is the only choice, but I believe there are benefits to both types. Let's begin by exploring the major differences between the two most common types of piping; there are others, but most are either illegal or outdated. Copper pipe comes in ten- and twenty-foot sticks or sections. It is rated by the wall thickness. The most common copper pipes are types L and M, the latter being the thickest and the most durable. Copper is joined together by copper couplings, which are sweated with a cleaning flux, solder and torch, providing an extremely solid and long lasting joint. P.V.C. pipe also comes in ten- and twenty-foot sticks. It is also rated by wall thickness. The only type still rated for use in water systems is Schedule Forty; there are others, but they are primarily used for sewer and drainage applications. P.V.C. comes in two types: P.V.C. for use with cold water and C.P.V.C. for use on hot water. They are not interchangeable. P.V.C. is joined with couplings and a fusion type glue. C.P.V.C. is joined using couplings and a filler glue. The joint on P.V.C. is usually fairly weak and needs support to keep from separating. Now let's look at price. Copper pipe is very expensive to purchase, and labor costs are usually at least three times that of P.V.C., but once installed properly, it will last indefinitely. P.V.C. is inexpensive and easy to install, but it can be easily damaged. In new homes, were cost is usually not a big factor, I highly recommend the use of copper. In existing homes, where cost or length of service is a problem, I recommend P.V.C. There is no doubt that copper pipe is the best; but, if installed properly, P.V.C. is a viable alternative for temporary or low cost use.

STUDENT BUSINESS LETTER 1

Letter of Complaint
By J. Johnson

1000 Brevard Rd.
Jackson Hole, MT 00000
February 21, 2002

Management
Lore's home Improvement Warhouse
P.O. Box 15988
Atlanta, GA 30353

Dear Management a Micro Wave I bought at Lore's in Jackson Hole on November 2, 2001. I know the date and price because when I buy something expensive, I save the recites. This week while trying to use my micro wave the turn plate refuse to turn around. And all my food turns out burned.
I would like to get a new micro wave to replace the one I have now. I paid $1600.00 for it. The model number is 32582100.
If you want to talk to me I can be riched at home. My number is: (000) 000-0000.

Sincerely,

J. Johnson

STUDENT BUSINESS LETTER 2

Request for Change of Work Schedule
By J. Johnson

1000 Brevard Rd.
Jackson Hole, MT 00000
February 26, 2002

Mr. Ralph Jacobs
Call-Mart
P.O. Box 749
Jackson Hole, MT 00000

Dear Mr. Jacobs,

I have been working for your componey as a cashier for two years. Working from 8:00to 12:00 noon. I'm a reliable and steady worker, and get along fine with other poeple. I'm writing to as for a change in my work hours. I want to take a class in book keeping which is given at 8:00am to 12: noon on Saturdays at the local college. If I could start work after 12:00 noon on Saturdays than I could take this class. Maby someone who's working evenings would like to work mornings on Saturday.
Idon't want to inconvenience you. I believe I will benefit your business if I was to do book keeping. I won't sign up for the class until I hear from you. You can call me at home at (000) 000–0000. or talk to me at work.

Sincerely,

J. Johnson

STUDENT CLASSIFICATION

A Powerful Team
By Michael Hadley

Three different classes of workers make up the restaurant business. These three classes have shaped this business as it is known today. The employees and managers both work inside the stores and are responsible for making the money. The office workers only work in the stores on special occasions and are responsible for managing the money. These three different jobs have a great effect on the way the business is run. In fact, without the employees, managers, and office workers, there would be no business at all.

The employee is considered to be the first class in a business. Most employees are teenagers making just above minimum wage on an hourly schedule. Just because they are the first class does not mean that they're not important. As a matter of fact, the employees are crucial to the business. They are the individuals that cook, clean, and deal directly with every customer. As people in the restaurant business know, dealing with the customer is the hardest task. For example, an employee must greet the customer and take his or her order. Then, the employee must rely on fellow employees to get the order correct and have it ready in time. Once the food is ready to serve, the employee must be friendly and the customer must be satisfied.

The second class to the restaurant business is the manager. The manager also has an important job. Because the manager has more authority and works longer hours, he or she makes more money. It is important to remember, however, that a manager's job is not any more important than an employee's. Most managers deal less with the customers and more with the employees. The manager must make sure the employees are doing their jobs correctly. The manager's job requirement is to train new employees, deal with the customer on special occasions, and make sure the store is operating the correct way. For example, if the bathrooms are dirty, then it is the manager's job to make sure they get cleaned. Also, if a customer has a problem, the manager must do his best to fix it.

The third and highest class in the restaurant business is the office workers. This includes the accountant, store supervisor, maintenance crew, and owner or operator. Their jobs are to make the paychecks, keep the restaurants in good condition, train the managers, and keep all the paperwork up to date. Office workers usually make the most money and have a higher education and degree. Although their job is very important to the business, these workers tend to deal with customers even less than the manager. However, on occasion an angry or pleased customer might go to the office to voice his or her opinion.

The employee, manager, and office worker are crucial to the restaurant business. They all have very different jobs, but they are of equal importance. The employee must make the customer happy and serve great food, the manager must make sure the employees are doing their job, and the office workers must keep the business going. Their jobs form a very powerful team of workers and make the business what it is.

STUDENT PROCESS

How to Make Tomato Sauce
By Rossano Cherubini

In Italy, since the times of the ancient Romans, cooking and eating have always been represented as an art rather than just satisfying the basic human need for food. Since then, Italian cuisine has been famous throughout the world as a traditional, simple and healthy one. The traditional Italian dish is pasta, and the indispensable element in pasta cooking is "La Pummarola," the tomato sauce. It is the base of all the so-called "red sauces," and it can be seasoned to suit personal tastes. However, the Italians usually say that the simplest is the best, and, of the many sauce recipes, this is a simple one. You will find that it will not be necessary to drive to the grocery store, because the things that you need are among the most common. In fact, the only ingredients needed to make this sauce are two pounds of tomatoes, an onion, two stalks of celery, and a carrot. Toward the end of the preparation, salt, pepper, and virgin olive oil are added for seasoning. The only equipment necessary is two saucepans, a strainer, a chopping knife, and a spoon. By following these simple steps, anyone can make the perfect Italian tomato sauce.

You should begin your sauce by preparing the vegetables, and for this you will need to use the chopping knife. First, peel one carrot and cut it lengthwise into strips. You will get four to six strips, depending on the size of the carrot. Second, you have to dice the strips into small cubes. Similarly, you dice two stalks of celery, trimming off the leafage. The onion, like the carrot, has to be peeled, but minced thinly rather than diced. Regarding the tomatoes, they should be soft and ripe for this recipe. You begin preparing the tomatoes by first washing them in cool running water. Second, placing the tomatoes with the stem up, you cut them in half from top to bottom and trim out the cores. Third, the tomatoes should be cut into quarters, and then diced. The carrot, onion, and celery are used and recommended not only for their complementary flavors, but also for the fact that they act together as a counter to the acidity of the tomatoes.

Now that all the ingredients are ready, you can start the actual cooking of the sauce. Take one of the two saucepans and put in the tomatoes so that they completely cover the bottom of the pan. Next, you can add the carrot, onion, and celery on top. You need to make sure that this is the exact sequence of vegetables in the pan and for a good reason: while cooking, the tomatoes will give off liquid and it is this liquid that will take the place of butter, which is normally used to sauté vegetables. On the other hand, if you put the carrot, onion or celery first, they would burn and stick to the bottom of the pan. Once all the vegetables are in the pan, you need to cover and cook slowly on a low heat for forty-five minutes until all the ingredients are soft. This may seem like a long time, but it is fundamental to allow the flavors of the tomatoes and those of the other vegetables to blend.

Once the sauce has been cooked for the given length of time and the vegetables are soft enough for mashing, you should be ready for the next step: straining the sauce. What you need now is the second saucepan and the strainer. First, place the strainer over the top of the saucepan. Second, you have to pour the vegetable mixture into the strainer. Third, you will want to use the spoon to press the mixture through the strainer so that as much as possible drains into the saucepan. You will have some of the mixture remaining in the strainer, but you can scrape the pulp from the outside bottom of the strainer and add it to the sauce. Now, all you have to do is reheat the sauce. While stirring slowly, add salt and pepper to taste, and two tablespoons of virgin olive oil. The sauce at this point has enough character to be served with any type of pasta, or, at your choice and with double or triple quantities, the sauce can be frozen in small portions and stored in your freezer. If this is the case, it will be always ready by only reheating it in a pan with a tablespoon of olive oil.

Finally, your sauce is ready to cover a steaming plate of spaghetti. At this point, in order to have a true Italian sauce, you need an Italian final touch: fresh basil. However, do not make the mistake of chopping it, because Italians believe that it would bring bad luck. You must break the leaves into small pieces with your fingers and put them in the sauce along with the salt, pepper, and olive oil. After you have done this, you need to let the sauce simmer for about five more minutes in order for the basil to lend its flavor. Of course, you can always use ready canned tomato sauces and artificial flavors, but you will miss the pleasure of cooking and a great taste that will really impress your guests. Buon Appetito!

STUDENT NARRATION

Fourteen Days of Uncertainty
By Heather Bridges

Life as a twelve year old was perfect, or so I thought. I was a carefree sixth grader. Okay, so I did worry a little, but they were all insignificant things like what lunch was going to be, if I was going to be late for school, which kickball team I would be on. Then one day everything changed. Life all of a sudden was not quite as happy anymore. Now it was tense, sad, and worry-filled.

All these uneasy feelings began when one Sunday morning I woke up and realized that my neighbor, Lucy, was at my house instead of my mom and dad. This, however, was not alarming to me because she was more than a neighbor. She was more like a grandmother to me and my brother. She was at the hospital the day I was born. Many days my brother and I resided at her house after school. However, this specific day she was not herself. The first thing she told me when I woke up, was that my dad was in the hospital. Although she attempted not to look overly worried, her face told it all. From her puffy, red eyes to her tense, nervous demeanor, it was impossible for her to hide the seriousness of what had happened. She told me that my mom was going to call when she was told more about the situation. Even though it had only been an hour-and-a-half until my mother called, it seemed like an eternity. She talked to Lucy first then me. Her voice was soft and shaky, as if she were crying. She told me that my dad had a heart attack earlier that morning and that everything should be fine. I did not know whether this was the whole truth, but I did know she was trying to assure me that it would all be okay. She knew as soon as she said those words that I would be comforted. For the next fourteen days I did not see my father at all. From what I understood, as soon as his condition was stabilized an ambulance took him to the Air Force Base Hospital. After all of the blood work and tests had been run, the doctors decided which procedure would be best. They decided to perform an angioplasty and give him medication instead of bypass surgery. This decision was based on his age. He was only forty years old. The angioplasty and medicine worked well, but over the next three years he was very uncertain about his health. This caused him to panic every time he had angina, which resulted in many trips to the emergency room and several two to three day stays in the hospital. All of this added extra stress on the whole family. Therefore, my brother and I tried our hardest to help around the house and not bother them too much.

All of this caused me to feel extremely uneasy about the stability of my family. I had never even imagined how it would be without having my dad around. The emotional, not to mention the financial, difficulties on my mother would have been like a huge black cloud hovering over her. So many horrible thoughts came to my mind during those fourteen days in particular. Even after he had the operation and came home, I still was not myself. Life was not the same anymore. Now I was more withdrawn from people and much quieter, which is something that I normally was not. I was very worried for quite a long time. For instance, every time I would hear sirens I would wonder if it was my dad in the ambulance. Guilt was another feeling I had. Every time I would go play with friends or just ride my bicycle around the block, I would think of how my dad was at home sick and could not do any of these things anymore.

It has been seven years since his first heart attack. During this time he had more heart-related problems. The doctors decided after all of these problems that bypass surgery was now a step that had to be taken. He had double-bypass surgery in January of 1995. Since then, his health has improved tremendously. We feel more at ease with his health today than we did five or six years ago. Therefore, my life, and his, are pretty much back to normal.

MEMO 1

Date: 8 March 1998
To: Margo Lippincott, A and E Construction
From: Ellen Donner, Assist. Man.
Subject: Late Shipment

As per your letter of 7 March 1998, permit me to say that we in management here at Cuzco Building and Supply are aware of the problems with your outgoing order which left the docks at approximately 0700 hours on 23 February, two days after our mutually agreed upon shipping schedule. Unfortunately, the matter did not come to our attention until receipt of your letter.

   Our Mr. Lindell in Accounts will be sending A and E a refund under separate cover within five business days as a form of apology for our screw-up. I still don't know how it happened, but I assure you that when I do heads will roll in due course. Kindly advise us if we can do anything further to make up for what happened. Attached please find a copy of the shipping form and inventory list for your records.

In closing, I would like to say that A and E Construction is a valued customer, and we hope that this matter will not tarnish future relations. Hoping to hear from you soon, I remain

Ellen Donner
Assist. Man.
Cuzco Building and Supply Co.

Enc.

MEMO 2

To: Everyone
From: Jocelyn Barnett
Date: August 1, 1998
Subject: Request for Supplies

We all have noticed that the copier has been out of toner of late. No doubt due to excessive use by members of Personnel who need a copier of their own. Production has also been using our copier when theirs is down and since many of their documents have dramatic all-black backgrounds, our toner is used up nearly three times as fast as usual. Personnel and Production need a copier and an additional copier, respectively. Using the copier here in Accounts Receivable only slows up our work schedule, as you can imagine, and those persons who are guilty know who they are and they should stop doing so immediately or the matter will be turned over to their supervisors right away. I hope to see this matter handled in a mature fashion. Thank you.

Jocelyn Barnett
Accounts

APPENDIX D

TRANSPARENCY MASTERS

CHAPTERS 1–12

WHY SHOULD I BECOME A GOOD WRITER?

E-mail messages are a standard means of communication in most workplaces.

Long-distance written communication is becoming more important.

Written communication skills can improve public speaking ability.

On-line courses in higher education may become a convenient option for students to receive degrees and gain valuable workforce skills—and all of the material must be submitted in writing.

Employers are searching for people with strong critical thinking skills, who can make well-reasoned decisions—written communication skills are one means of developing better critical thinking ability.

Writing for enjoyment may improve a person's quality of life by opening up a creative outlet for expressing experiences, feelings, and ideas in a unique way.

INVENTION STRATEGIES/
PREWRITING TECHNIQUES

Freewriting

Write without stopping and without worrying about punctuation and grammar.

Focused Freewriting

Write on a specific topic without stopping.

Blind Freewriting

Turn off your computer monitor and freewrite.

Clustering

(also known as "Bubbling" and "Mapping") Begin with topic in the center of the page; write down every idea that occurs to you; group related thoughts and images by connecting them with lines. Strive to fill the page quickly.

Listing

Make a list down a fresh page of all ideas that occur to you without worrying about creating complete sentences.

Doodling

For visual learners, a combination of drawing and jotting down words can free creativity.

Taping

For auditory learners, recording associative ideas on a topic on a hand-held tape recorder (voice activated is useful) and then playing back the tape can be an effective method of idea generation.

Harcourt, Inc.

WHY SHOULD I USE INVENTION STRATEGIES/ PREWRITING TECHNIQUES?

- Prewriting can be an effective means to break writer's block.

- It is a means to "finding your interest" within an assigned topic.

- It may help you uncover unverbalized opinions and ideas.

- It will help you to create a topic sentence or thesis statement that you have interest in proving.

- It will help you generate supporting details to support your topic sentence or thesis.

- It may be a means to connect idea clusters quickly, which may eventually become paragraphs.

- Prewriting can release dormant creativity.

- It can also cause you to pay attention to details that you would normally filter out.

AN EXAMPLE OF
FREEWRITING FOR A
DEFINITION PARAGRAPH

Good actions. that may need to be defined. For example, are apologies good action? giving gifts? Taking care of animals? Doing things that make others feel good? Or is it only when you are helping others who are in need? I've never even questioned this before. I'm stuck. Wahere was I? It seems to me that many actions that we do which we name "good" are just cultural expectations that we are tring to satisfy . . . .Christimas gifts, tithing, volunteer work. It seems that it must have something to do with the spirit or quality of heart in which something is don. Am I rigtht about that? The mindfulness, selflessness. And then if one starts to regret the selfless action because it is not appresiated, does it become the opposite of a good action? Telling the truth when it will have repercussions on oneself. Giving when it will cause personal sacrifices. Giving time to others rather than to one's own pursuits. But if one is only doing these things to be thought of as a good person . . . !!!! Doesn't that negate the good action? Each day lived to the fullest is a good action, i think. A person for who good actions are integral in their lives may have trouble remembering their good actions because it is a way of live for them. And they don't expect a reward. If you are paid for doing something good, is it still a good action? not doing a bad action that someone wants to do might be considered a good action.

FINAL PARAGRAPH DRAWN
FROM FREEWRITING

Many people I talk to refer to "good actions" or "good works" with suggestion that we have a simple, common definition. However, I realized that attempting a definition of "good actions" can be very slippery indeed. First, we need to realize that many of the things we may do which make us feel good about ourselves are not necessarily good actions. We actually do them because of cultural expectations. Some examples of these actions might be giving gifts for birthdays or holidays, giving blood, giving money in the offering plate each Sunday, and coaching a Little League team. Second, if one is doing a good action in order to be thought of as a good person by one's friends, family, or community, then the action in itself may not be purely good. One example from my experience is the time I gave a dollar to a homeless man which made me a hero with my friends. The truth is, I had five dollars in my pocket. I could have given the homeless man all of my money, but I didn't think he deserved it. Third, if one ends up regretting a good action because it wasn't appreciated properly, one's good action becomes tainted. I once gave my jacket to a classmate who was cold, and she told her friends that my jacket had a bad smell. I was angry that she didn't appreciate my selflessness and talked badly about her for a year after that. The conclusion that I have come to is that good actions must be deeds which help others, which are a personal sacrifice, and which are done without desire for reward or thanks.

THE ELEMENTS OF GOOD WRITING

Purpose

Why am I writing?

What do I wish to prove or disprove?

Am I *explaining* a concept, *defining* an idea, *classifying* information, *comparing* two topics to find similarities or differences, *showing how to do* a project, *describing* an event, *narrating* a story, or *showing the causes or effects* of a course of action?

Audience

Whom am I writing to?

Who most needs to receive the information I have to offer?

What is the best approach for reaching these readers?

Prewriting

What do I already know about the topic?

(*Freewriting, journal writing, brainstorming,* and *clustering*)

What can I find out? (*Researching*)

What are the main points I should cover? (*Outlining*)

Unity

What is my *thesis*?

What is the *topic sentence* of each paragraph?

Do the topic sentences relate to the thesis?

Do the sentences in each paragraph clearly expand the topic sentences?

Coherence

How have I *organized* my information?

Is the progression of my thoughts *logical* and *clear*?

Have I provided enough *transitional words and phrases* to help readers understand the relationship of each idea to the others?

Harcourt, Inc.

FINDING THE SUBJECT OF A SENTENCE 1

1. Subjects usually answer, "Who or what is the sentence about?"

   Tameka washed her new Mazda after work.

   Question: Who/what is the sentence about?
   Answer: Tameka.

2. Subjects often come early in the sentence. In addition, a subject is often

   a noun: a word that names persons, places, or things and can function as a subject, an object, or a possessive in the sentence

   or a pronoun: a word used to take the place of a noun such as *I, you, he, she, it, we, they.*

   **The *nozzle* on the first sprayer Tameka
   tried was broken.**

   ***She* moved the car into another stall
   and tried again.**

3. **Noun and pronoun subjects can be modified by an adjective:**

   a word that modifies (describes or limits) a noun or pronoun.

   **The new, lipstick-red *Mazda* glistened
   as it dried in the bright sun.**

   **New and lipstick-red are adjectives
   modifying Mazda.**

4. The subject can be a compound:

   two or more nouns or pronouns joined together by *and, or, either/or,* or *neither/nor.*

   ***Tameka* and *Raita* took a drive later
   that afternoon.**

   **Neither the *heat* nor the *traffic* could
   spoil their mood.**

Harcourt, Inc.

FINDING THE SUBJECT OF A SENTENCE 2

Since a subject can never be found in a prepositional phrase (a group of words containing a preposition and an object of the preposition with its modifiers), the subject of a sentence is easier to detect if the prepositional phrases are deleted.

**After the sun went down, _Tonio_ took his friend
to a diner for a hamburger.**

Sun, diner, and **hamburger** cannot be subjects because they are objects of prepositional phrases.

Since the subject of a sentence cannot be found in an appositive (a word or group of words that gives extra information about a noun), deleting appositives can make it easier to find the subject.

**_Marketa,_ a Czech college student, will be
coming to live with us.**

A Czech college student is an appositive for **Marketa** because it gives extra information about her.

To find the subject of questions, change the question to a statement.

When did _Tonio_ meet Janessa?

Tonio met Janessa when they were in high school.

If a sentence that is not a question begins with a verb and gives a command, the subject of the sentence is an understood (although it is not written) **you.**

Take out the garbage right this minute.

(You) take out the garbage right this minute.

Since **here** and **there** can never be subjects, ask yourself what the sentence is about.

Here are the _magic markers_ I was looking for.

(The _magic markers_ I was looking for are here.)

Harcourt, Inc.

FINDING VERBS
IN SENTENCES

After you have located the subject of any given sentence, you should have no trouble finding the verb if you pay attention to these three types:

action verbs   These verbs tell us what the subject is doing and when the action occurs.

Mike **drove** at least seventy miles to work each week day last year. Mike is the subject. What did he do? Drive. When? In the past.

linking verbs   These verbs link the subject to one or more words which identify and/or describe the subject.

Martha Fuller **has become** a fine surgeon at Mercy Hospital.

Rodney **is feeling** confident about his chances of being hired.

I **am** really hungry.

Martha Fuller can be renamed by the phrase *a fine surgeon.*

Confident describes some aspect of the subject *Rodney.*

Really hungry describes the state of being for the subject *I.*

(Some common linking verbs are: *feel, grow, look, seem, appear,* and all forms of the verb *to be.*)

helping verbs   These verbs are used to help the main verb express time or special meaning.

Eve **was reading** in the Student Union on her lunch hour.

They **will be going** to Mexico for Spring Break.

I **have taken** the driver's test twice already.

Was is a helping verb for the main verb to read and helps it to describe continuous action in the past.

Will be are helping verbs for the main verb *to go* and help it to describe continuous action in the future.

Have is a helping verb for the main verb *to take* and helps it to describe finished action in the past with reference to the present.

MAKING SUBJECTS AND
VERBS AGREE 1

Subject-verb agreement with pronouns.

Pay attention to present tenses, especially when combined with third-person singular pronouns *he, she,* or *it.*

> **I *love* watching old movies, but not Eddie. He *loves* action flicks.**

Subject-verb agreement with *do* and *be*.

Use *does, is,* and *was* with third-person singular pronouns *he, she,* and *it* and singular nouns.

> **She *does* enjoy skiing although she *is* not very experienced.**

> **When he *was* younger, Ron *was* a member of the ski club.**

Subject-verb agreement with hard-to-find subjects.

Subjects are not found in prepositional or appositive phrases.
Subjects can be found after the verb in sentences beginning with *here* or *there* and in questions.

> **There *are* several *things* I needed to talk about with
> Mary, president of the literacy council.**

Subject-verb agreement with group nouns.

A group noun such as *audience, crowd,* or *team* takes a singular verb if the noun acts as a unit; it takes a plural verb if the members of the group act independently.

> **My family *is* Australian.**

> **The association *are voting* on the important proposal tomorrow.**

MAKING SUBJECTS AND VERBS AGREE 2

Subject-verb agreement with indefinite pronouns

Indefinite pronouns ending in -one, -thing, or -body take a singular verb.

Somebody *has taken* my favorite pen.

***Does* anyone *know* who it was?**

Indefinite pronouns *both, few, many* and *several* take a plural verb.

Few of my childhood friends *have* children of their own.

Many of us *are hoping* to get good news.

Indefinite pronouns *any, all, more, most, none,* and *some* take either a singular or a plural verb depending on the meaning of the sentence.

The apples have some soft spots. Most *need* to be thrown out.

The salt is damp. Most *is* unusable.

Subject-verb agreement with compound subjects

Use a plural verb with compound subjects joined by *and* unless the two subjects compose a single unit.

The celery and green pepper *are* in the refrigerator.

The mortar and pestle *is made* of black marble.

Use either a singular or a plural verb with compound subjects joined by *or, nor, either, either/or, neither, neither/nor, not only/but also*—the verb should agree with the subject closest to it.

**Neither the magazines in the living room nor this magazine
on the table *contains* the article I am looking for.**

John or the Robinsons *are planning* to drive us home.

Harcourt, Inc.

CORRECTING THE FRAGMENT
IN SIMPLE SENTENCES 1

A fragment is a piece of a sentence.

Going out with a bang rather than a whimper.

To be or not to be.

Sally our neighbor across the hall.

At midnight.

Swimming, skiing, and hiking scenic trails.

Is better than nothing.

A fragment can be corrected by adding the missing parts of the sentence.

Going out with a bang rather than a whimper, *Rhonda spent her entire last paycheck on a party for her close friends.*

"To be or not to be," *that is the question Hamlet made famous.*

Sally, our neighbor across the hall, *has invited us to dinner.*

***Sandi thought she heard music* at midnight.**

***David likes* swimming, skiing, and hiking scenic trails.**

***It* is better than nothing.**

A fragment can sometimes be corrected by being added to the complete sentence before it or the complete sentence following it.

Most people today think of laundry as drudgery. *Even with the use of automatic washers and dryers. Only several decades ago.* Women were expected to set aside an entire day each week to do the laundry. Now that's drudgery!

Most people today think of laundry as drudgery, even with the use of automatic washers and dryers. Only several decades ago, women were expected to set aside an entire day each week to do laundry. Now that's drudgery!

CORRECTING THE FRAGMENT IN SIMPLE SENTENCES 2

Fragments are often made up of phrases. A **phrase** is a group of words that belongs together but does not make a complete sentence.

Noun phrase

A noun phrase is a group of words containing a noun and its modifiers.

> **The _gorgeous midsummer sunset_ lingered for an hour.**

Prepositional phrase

A prepositional phrase is a group of words beginning with a preposition and containing an object and possibly modifiers.

> **_After a relaxing and filling dinner_, four of us went walking.**

Verb phrase

A verb phrase is the main verb along with its helping verbs (auxiliary verbs). It is the complete verb of a sentence.

> **By next winter, Sam _will have been traveling_ in Asia for nearly eighteen months.**

CORRECTING THE FRAGMENT
IN SIMPLE SENTENCES 3

Participial phrase

A participial phrase is a participle plus its nouns and modifiers. A participle is often a present form of a verb ending in *-ing* or a past form of a verb ending in *-ed*. A participial phrase **functions as an adjective** in a sentence.

Running as fast as he could to the ice cream truck, **the child slipped and fell.**

That woman, *reading a poetry magazine,* **is Ezra's aunt Linda.**

Utterly exhausted, **the soccer team rode the bus in silence.**

Gerund phrase

A gerund phrase is a gerund plus its nouns and modifiers. A gerund is a present form of a verb ending in *-ing*. It can be distinguished from a participial phrase by its function: a gerund phrase **functions as a noun** in a sentence.

Running races **can be exciting. (Subject)**

I enjoy *reading poetry magazines.* **(Object)**

Infinitive phrase

An infinitive phrase is an infinitive plus its nouns and modifiers. An infinitive is formed by the word *to* plus the base form of the verb. An infinitive phrase can **function as a noun, an adjective, or an adverb** in a sentence. Note: the word *to* can also be a preposition. Look for the base form of a verb following *to* in order to make sure it is an infinitive.

Macy hates *to sleep* **on the floor. (Noun/Object)**

Art collected the bills *to be mailed* **immediately. (Adjective)**

To be truthful, **no one in the department wants that job. (Adverb)**

COMBINING SENTENCES USING THE THREE METHODS OF COORDINATION

Coordination is the joining of two sentences, known as **independent clauses,** which are related and contain ideas of equal importance.

A **compound sentence** is a sentence composed of two independent clauses joined by means of coordination.

There are three methods of coordination . . .

1. Use a comma and a coordinating conjunction *(and, but, for, nor, or, yet, so)* between the independent clauses.

2. Use a semicolon, an adverbial conjunction, and a comma between the two independent clauses.

3. Use only a semicolon between two independent clauses.

Emma wanted to go to the basketball game.

She needed a ride. (Two independent clauses)

**Emma wanted to go to the basketball game, *but* she needed a ride.
(Comma and coordinating conjunction)**

**Emma wanted to go to the game, *and* she needed a ride.
(Comma and coordinating conjunction)**

**Emma wanted to go to the game; *however,* she needed a ride.
(Semicolon, adverbial conjunction, and comma)**

**Emma wanted to go to the basketball game; she needed a ride.
(Semicolon only)**

COMBINING SENTENCES USING SUBORDINATION

Subordination is the joining of two clauses containing ideas that are not equally important.

The main point of the sentence is contained in the **independent clause,** and the less important point is contained in the **dependent clause.**

These clauses are joined by means of

subordinating conjunctions (*after, since, because, although, until, unless,* etc.)

and **relative pronouns** (*who, whose, whom, which, that*)

Sentences joined through subordination are called **complex sentences.**

Rodney has a great analytical mind.
He will be a good engineer. (Two independent clauses)

<u>Because</u> Rodney has a great analytical mind, **he will be a good engineer.**
(Subordinating conjunction)

Rodney, *<u>who</u> has a great analytical mind,* **will be a good engineer.**
(Relative pronoun)

CORRECTING THE RUN-ON

A run-on is a sentence in which two independent clauses have been combined incorrectly.

There are three common types of run-ons:

The **fused run-on**	The fused run-on is a sentence in which two independent clauses are joined without any punctuation or coordinating conjunctions between them.
The **comma splice**	The comma splice is a sentence in which two independent clauses have been joined using a comma but without using a coordinating conjunction.
The **"and" run-on**	The "and" run-on is a sentence in which two or more independent clauses have been joined using "and" (or another coordinating conjunction) but without using a comma(s).

Buying a house is a big step it can also be an important investment.
(Fused run-on)

Make sure you tour the house several times, many consumer advocates recommend flushing the toilets and running the faucets.
(Comma splice)

Do not sign a contract without getting a building inspection and it is a good idea to apply for pre-approval for your loan and many home buyers are embarrassed to take advantage of a final walk-through before closing the deal. ("And" run-on)

MNEMONIC DEVICES 1

FANBOYS:

The Coordinating Conjunctions

, **F** or

, **A** nd

, **N** or

, **B** ut

, **O** r

, **Y** et

, **S** o

MNEMONIC DEVICES 2

TIA WAS A WIT:

A Few Subordinating Conjunctions

T hat

I f

A lthough

W hen

A s

S ince

A fter

W hen

I nstead

T hough

MNEMONIC DEVICES 3

SOME TANS ARE HOT:
A Few Adverbial Sentence Modifiers

S uddenly,

O n the one hand,

M oreover,

E ventually,

T hirdly,

A dditionally,

N evertheless,

S imilarly,

A lso,

R ecently,

E mphatically,

H owever,

O n the other hand,

T herefore,

Harcourt, Inc.

MEMORY DEVICES FOR SENTENCE PATTERNS

IC = Independent Clause
DC = Dependent Clause
FANBOYS = Coordinating Conjunction
AM = Adverbial Sentence Modifier
Comma = ,
Semicolon = ;

Pattern 1:

IC + comma + FANBOYS + IC .

> **The best man dropped the ring, and everyone
> in the congregation stifled giggles.**

Pattern 2:

DC + comma + IC .

> **When the best man dropped the ring, the congregation stifled giggles.**

Pattern 3:

IC + DC .

> **The congregation stifled giggles when the best man dropped the ring.**

Pattern 4:

IC + semicolon + AM + comma + IC .

> **The best man dropped the ring; therefore, the entire
> congregation stifled giggles.**

Harcourt, Inc.

MAKING SENTENCE PARTS WORK TOGETHER: PRONOUNS 1

Pronouns can change form depending on whether they are being used as subjects, objects, possessives, or reflexives.

Pronouns in the **subjective** or **nominative case** are not only the subjects of sentences. They can also be the subjects of dependent clauses (noun clauses, adjective clauses, and adverb clauses) and absolute participial phrases (phrases that contain a subject).

Singular	I, you, he, she, it, who
Plural	we, you, they, who

A pronoun in the **objective case** can be the direct object of an independent or dependent clause, or the object of a phrase (prepositional, infinitive, gerund, or participial).

Singular	me, you, him, her, it, whom
Plural	us, you, them, whom

Pronouns in the **possessive case** show possession and act as adjectives within the sentence.

Singular	my/mine, you/yours, his, her, its, whose
Plural	our/ours, your/yours, their/theirs, whose

Pronouns in the **reflexive case** show action returning or being reflected upon its subject.

Singular	myself, yourself, himself, herself, itself
Plural	ourselves, yourselves, themselves

MAKING SENTENCE PARTS WORK TOGETHER: PRONOUNS 2

Special cases of pronoun agreement

Comparisons   When pronouns are used in a comparison, complete the comparison to find out whether the nominative or the objective case is appropriate.

Nikita is much better at learning new languages than I/me.

Nikita is much better at learning new languages than **I am.**

Compound constructions   When pronouns are used in a compound construction, take out one of the elements of the compound and use the pronoun that makes sense by itself.

After she/her and I/me left for the lecture, our father called.

After **she** left for the lecture, our father called.

After **I** left for the lecture, our father called.

Who/whom constructions   When *who* or *whom* is in a clause, cross out everything but the clause containing *who* or *whom* to find out how it functions in the clause (Subject of clause or phrase? Object of clause or phrase?)

That poet who/whom I told you about just published a new collection.

who/whom I told you about

I told you **about who/whom**

about **whom** (object of preposition—use objective case)

That poet **whom** I told you about just published a new collection.

Harcourt, Inc.

MAKING SENTENCE PARTS WORK TOGETHER: PRONOUNS 3

An **antecedent** is a word or words that a pronoun replaces.

The living room **furniture** we wanted was finally on sale.
It cost only a third of its original price.

1. A pronoun must agree in **number** (singular or plural) with any other word to which it refers.

The **lobbyists** never tired although **they** often wondered
if **their** efforts were appreciated.

2. A pronoun must agree with its antecedent in **person.** In other words, don't mix *I, you, one,* and *they.*

You really ought to travel. One cannot imagine the
experiences that are in store for them. (faulty)

You really ought to travel. **You** cannot imagine the
experiences in store for **you.**

3. The antecedent of a pronoun should not be **missing, ambiguous, or repetitious.**

They always say, "Better safe than sorry." (Who are "they"?)
An old adage claims that people are "better safe than sorry."
Melissa and her mom are volunteering for Habitat for Humanity these days.
She said **she** really feels good about the work **they** are doing. (Which woman
said she feels good? Whose work does she feel good about—
the organization's or the mother and daughter's?)
Melissa and her mom are volunteering for Habitat for Humanity these days.
Melissa says **she** feels good about the work **Habitat** is doing.

MAKING SENTENCE PARTS WORK TOGETHER: PARALLEL STRUCTURE AND MODIFIERS 1

Parallel structure

Words in a series should be the same parts of speech.

> I wanted to see the **sunset,** the **constellations,** or the **moon rise** over the lake.
> (nouns mixed with finite verb)

Phrases in a series should be the same kinds of phrases (infinitive, verb, noun, prepositional, gerund, or participial)

> The girls had a ball **sleeping** in bunk beds, **making** pancakes,
> and **went out** looking for wild herbs in the woods.
> (gerund phrases mixed with finite verb—delete *went out*)

Clauses in a series should not be mixed with phrases.

> I told him **about the cabin, about the trip,** and **what happened** when John
> overturned the canoe. (prepositional phrases mixed with a noun clause)

MAKING SENTENCE PARTS WORK TOGETHER: PARALLEL STRUCTURE AND MODIFIERS 2

A **modifier** is a word or group of words that functions as an adjective or adverb.

A **misplaced modifier** is a word or group of words that has been placed in a **wrong, awkward,** or **ambiguous position.**

> The guests seemed to have the goal **to practically eat**
> my parents out of house and home.

A **dangling modifier** is a modifier without a word, phrase, or clause that the modifier can describe.

> Hanging on her every word, the door burst open
> and startled the rapt audience.

> **Hanging** on the lecturer's every word, the **audience**
> was startled when the door burst open.

Harcourt, Inc.

PRACTICING MORE WITH VERBS 1

The principal parts of verbs:

Base Form
(to + verb, also called the *infinitive*)

regular verb: irregular verb:
to **enjoy**   to **grow**

Past Tense
(in regular verbs, just add *-ed;* the past tense of
irregular verbs will *not* be formed by adding *-ed*)

enjoyed   **grew**

Past Participle
(in the active voice, it is preceded by *have*,
***has*, or *had*; in regular verbs, the past tense**
and past participle are the same)

enjoyed   **grown**

Present Participle
(base form + *-ing*)

enjoying   **growing**

PRACTICING MORE WITH VERBS 2

What do present verb tenses mean?

Present (present tense form of the verb/add *-s* or *-es* for third person singular)   The present tense is used to show actions happening now and facts/actions that are always true.

His son **grows** bigger each time I see him.

Present Continuous (*am/is/are* + present participle)   Use the present continuous to describe most actions occurring in the present moment, especially actions that are constant or ongoing.

Tom **is growing** fond of cycling.

Present Perfect (*have/has* + past participle)   Use present perfect to explain a discreet action which began in the past and is ending or continuing in the present. It can describe an event that has just taken place, or an action in which the time is indefinite.

I **have grown** several types of herbs this summer.
(Action began in the past and is still current)

Present Perfect Continuous (*have/has* + *been* + present participle)   Use present perfect continuous when the continuous or constant action which began in the past is still going on.

Selene **has been growing** tomatoes in her basement since January.

PRACTICING MORE WITH VERBS 3

What do past verb tenses mean?

Past (past form of verb)   Use past tense to describe most actions which occurred in the past.

Hillary **read** *War and Peace* last month.

Past Continuous (*was/were* + present participle)   Use past continuous to describe a continuous or constant action which occured in the past. It is often used in conjunction with a past tense verb.

Lino **was going** into the health food store when he **saw** his old high school buddy.

Past Perfect (*had* + past participle)   Use past perfect to describe an action which occurred prior to another past action. It is often used in conjunction with a past tense verb.

Janine **had taken** the ACT two months before she **entered** college.

Past Perfect Continuous (*had* + *been* + present participle)   Use the past perfect continuous tense to describe a continuous or constant action (belief, fact) that occurred in the past but ended due to another action that occurred in the more recent past.

Rick **had been going** to night school for two years when
he **received** a scholarship to Penn State.

PRACTICING MORE WITH VERBS 4

What do future verb tenses mean?

Future (*will/shall* + base form of the verb)   Use the future to describe most actions that will occur at a later time.

Dominique **will travel** back to her homeland in June.

Future Continuous (*will/shall* + *be* + present participle)   Use future continuous to describe an action which will be continuous or constant at a later time.

She **will be flying** on TWA.

Future Perfect (*will/shall* + *have* + past participle)   Use future perfect to describe an action that will be completed by a given time in the future.

The eighteen-year-old Czech student **will have completed** two years of advanced language study by the time she returns home.

Future Perfect Continuous (*will/shall* + *have* + *been* + present participle)   Use the future perfect continuous tense to describe a constant or continuous action which began at a time prior to the point in the future referred to.

At that time, she **will have been studying** English for a total of eight years.

USING CORRECT CAPITALIZATION AND PUNCTUATION 1

Capitalize the first word of every sentence.

Don't listen to him. **He** is just jealous. **Ignore** him.

Capitalize the names of specific things and places.

We went to **Devil's Den** over the holidays and stayed over night
by the **Buffalo River** at **Thunderbird Inn.**

Capitalize the days of the week, months, and holidays, but don't capitalize the names of the seasons.

I can't believe that **Wednesday** is the first day of **spring.**

Capitalize the names of all languages, nationalities, races, religions, deities, and sacred terms.

I have studied **Spanish, Greek,** and **Hebrew.**

Capitalize the first word and every important word in a title. Do not capitalize articles, prepositions, or short connecting words in a title.

The Complete Works of William Shakespeare

Capitalize the first word of a direct quotation.

My sister shouted, **"Hold** that thought!"

Capitalize historical events, periods, and documents.

We studied Picasso's **Blue Period** last night.

Capitalize the words north, south, east, and west when they are used as places rather than as directions.

Lonnie was born in the **Midwest,** but he is now living on the **East Coast.**

USING CORRECT CAPITALIZATION AND PUNCTUATION 2

Using commas

Use a comma to separate items in a series.

> The supply list requested **large mailing envelopes, packing tape, a stapler, and bubble wrap.**

When an address or date occurs in a sentence, each part is treated like an item in a series. A comma is put after each item, including the last.

> On **May 14, 1998,** in **Reno, Nevada,** my brother was married.

A group of adjectives may not be regarded as a series if some of the words "go together." You can test this by putting *and* between each item. If you can, use a comma.

> The child discovered the **fragile, pale blue** egg beside the rain gutter.

Use a comma to follow introductory words, expressions, phrases, or clauses.

> **As you well know,** I enjoy talking on the phone.

Use commas surrounding a word, phrase, or clause when the word or group of words interrupts the main idea.

> My mother, **the perfectionist,** uses a razorblade to chop the garlic for spaghetti sauce.

Use commas around nouns in direct address.

> **Martin,** could we plan on a general staff meeting for next Monday?

Use a comma to set off exact words spoken in dialogue.

> "It seems crazy," **said Greg,** "not to invest in flood insurance."

Harcourt
College Publishers

Where Learning Comes to Life

TECHNOLOGY

Technology is changing the learning experience, by increasing the power of your textbook and other learning materials; by allowing you to access more information, more quickly; and by bringing a wider array of choices in your course and content information sources.

Harcourt College Publishers has developed the most comprehensive Web sites, e-books, and electronic learning materials on the market to help you use technology to achieve your goals.

PARTNERS IN LEARNING

Harcourt partners with other companies to make technology work for you and to supply the learning resources you want and need. More importantly, Harcourt and its partners provide avenues to help you reduce your research time of numerous information sources.

Harcourt College Publishers and its partners offer increased opportunities to enhance your learning resources and address your learning style. With quick access to chapter-specific Web sites and e-books . . . from interactive study materials to quizzing, testing, and career advice . . . Harcourt and its partners bring learning to life.

Harcourt's partnership with Digital:Convergence™ brings :CRQ™ technology and the :CueCat™ reader to you and allows Harcourt to provide you with a complete and dynamic list of resources designed to help you achieve your learning goals. You can download the free :CRQ software from www.crq.com. Visit any of the 7,100 RadioShack stores nationwide to obtain a free :CueCat reader. Just swipe the cue with the :CueCat reader to view a list of Harcourt's partners and Harcourt's print and electronic learning solutions.

C 62 00 00 00 00 00 25 20L

http://www.harcourtcollege.com/partners